JO FLETCHER

Pitman 200
Reporting

Pitman

PITMAN PUBLISHING LIMITED
128 Long Acre, London WC2E 9AN

A Longman Group Company

First published in Great Britain 1979
Second Edition 1986
Reprinted 1986

British Library Cataloguing in Publication Data
Reporting style.—2nd ed.—
(Pitman 2000 shorthand)
1. Shorthand—Pitman—Examinations, questions, etc.
653′.4242′076 Z56.2.P/

Text set in 10/12 pt Linotron Century
Printed and bound in Great Britain
at The Bath Press, Avon

ISBN 0 273 02508 2

Contents

Longhand Keys to Reading and Writing Practice

Preface

This book is aimed at all those students of Pitman 2000 Shorthand with a writing speed of 120 wam who wish to write shorthand at verbatim levels (180–200 wam). The book does this by increasing the student's shorthand knowledge and practising the methods of achieving higher speeds.

Reporting Style 2nd edition contains a brief extension of shorthand theory and an increase in the number of short forms, further development of phrasing and intersecting, and a few special outlines for distinguishing some words that resemble one another because of their consonantal structure. Presented in 12 units, each unit contains shorthand material to practise the theory of each unit. Longhand keys, counted in tens for dictation, appear after Unit 12.

All material in the book has been carefully selected to present a wide range of content and graded to provide practice for all the new principles of theory and phrasing. Any new advanced princples of phrasing introduced follow the relevant theory.

Teachers should use the book once students have reached a speed of 120 wam—and once students have a thorough knowledge of all the principles of phrasing since many of these principles are used in the shorthand passages—it is not intended for shorthand-writing office workers. (It may be best to use the shorthand passage provided for each unit only when practising the theory learnt in that unit.)

As a guide, for each unit the student should learn thoroughly all the theory; practise all the outlines, short forms, distinguishing outlines and phrases.

Reading and Writing passages should be read several times and checked in the longhand if the student has difficulties with any outlines. The student's shorthand should also be monitored to check all new theory is being used.

Shorthand material should be read aloud, reread by the student several times until a reading speed of twice the dictation speed is attained and then copied from timed dictation several times, with an increase in speed each time. The material should then be taken down from dictation without reference to the text. The students should compare their shorthand with that in the book and practise any incorrect outlines. Once students have mastered the shorthand appearing in each unit, they should move to the next.

It should be stated that rapid advancement of speed is usually achieved once all the principles of theory and phrasing have been learnt. It is quite satisfactory to maintain speed after completing each unit—rapid speed increase will occur after completion of the course.

The use of dictation cassettes in this course is recommended since these will not only provide vocal variety but allow the teacher to study the shorthand writing habits of the students.

To aid the student it is best to read only the shorthand in this book for practice—not printed shorthand—so that the new principles of shorthand and phrasing are firmly lodged in the student's mind.

Janet Job and Bert Canning

Unit One

Abbreviated W

A small semicircle, written ..⊃.., is used initially as an abbreviation for **W** at the beginning of **K, G, M** and upward and downward **R.** The small semicircle is always read first:

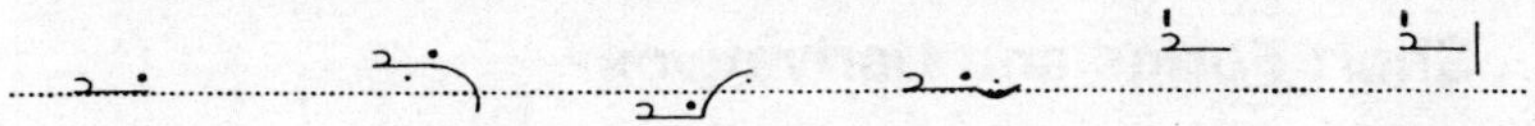

week/weak weaker weekly weekend walk walked

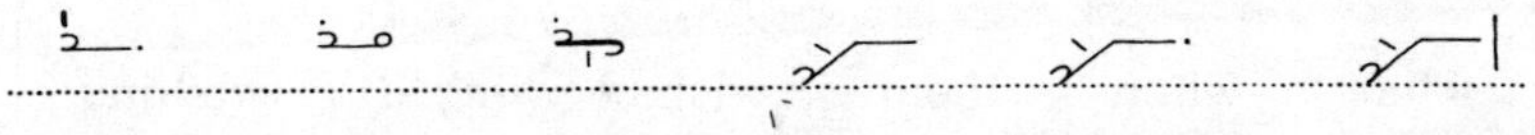

walking wax wagon work working worked

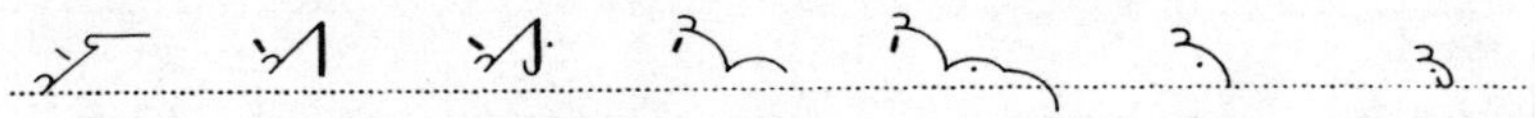

worker ward warden warm warmer were weren't

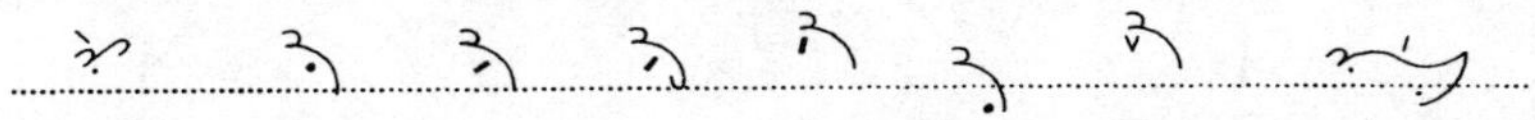

warrant wear wore worn war weir wire womanish

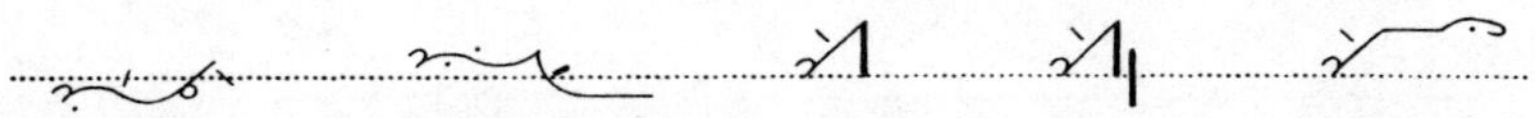

womanhood womenfolk word worded workmen

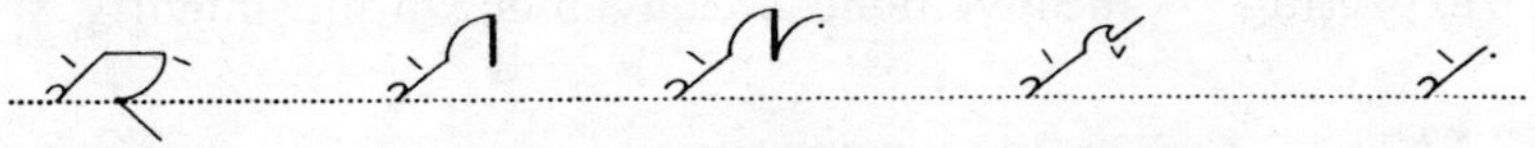

workshop world worldly worldwide worry

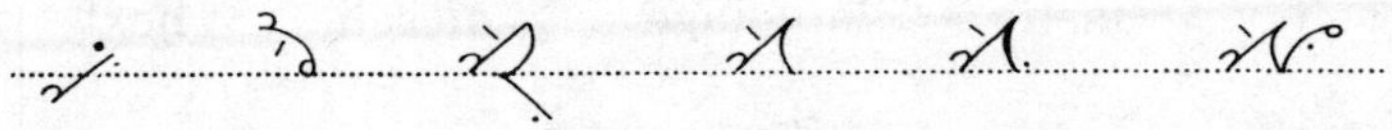

weary worse worship worth worthy worthless

When **W** is preceded by a vowel, the stroke **W**  must be used:

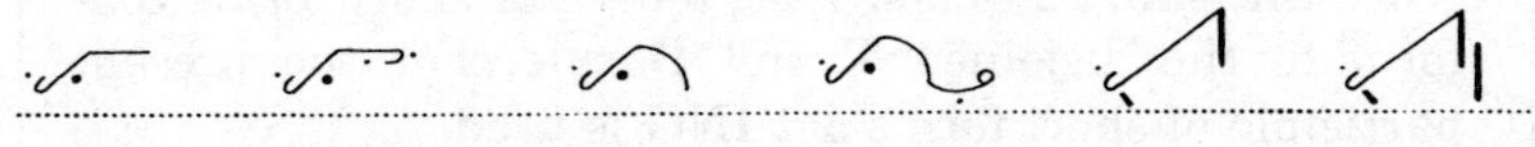

awake awakening aware awareness award awarded

Distinguishing Outlines

The English language contains many words which have a similar consonantal structure. Provision is made in this Pitman 2000 Shorthand Reporting Style for the easy differentiation of some of these words that might otherwise be confused, by the use of distinguishing outlines so that the writers of this system will have no difficulty either in the writing or in the transcription of these similarly constructed words.

Note: The outline for the word **woman** is written in first position 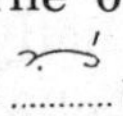 to distinguish it from **women** .

Short Forms and Derivatives

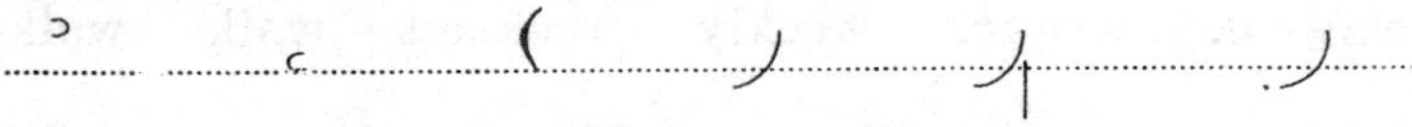

what when them wish wished wishing

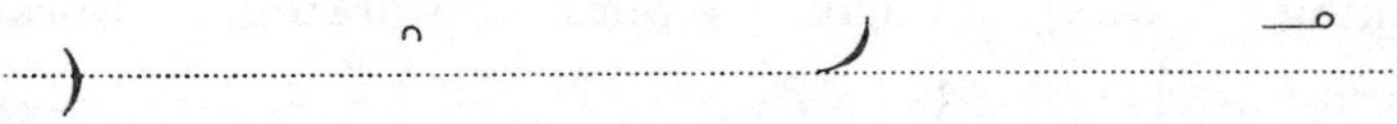

whose beyond usual/usually because

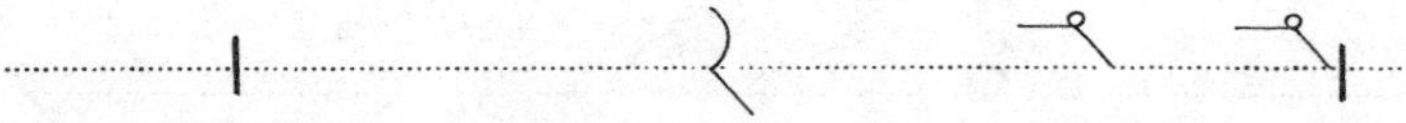

difference/different especial/especially expect expected

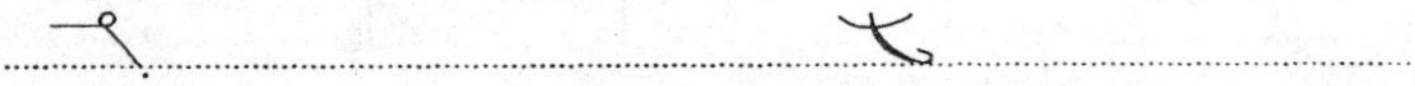

expecting inconvenience/inconvenient/inconveniently

himself itself language myself next

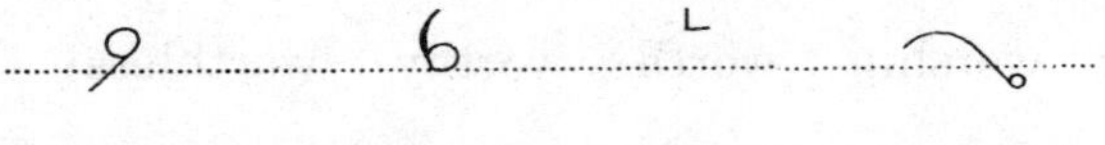

ourselves themselves why impossible

Note on Short Forms: Past tenses of short forms conform to the disjoined **T** and **D** rule. For the present participle of short forms dot **ING** is used.

Phrases

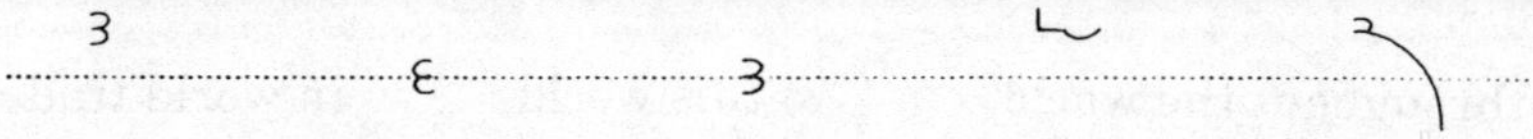

what you when you would you why not were there

man and woman men and women what is the matter

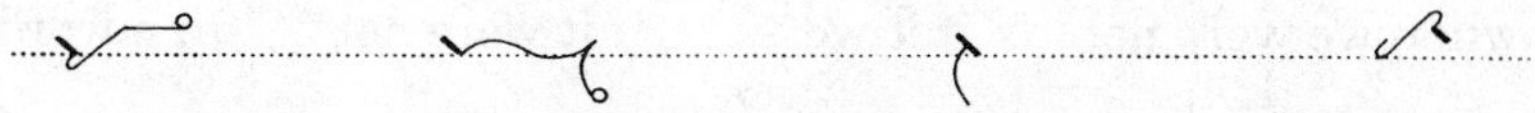

two weeks two months two or three one or two

or two too much too many too little

Phrasing Principles

The initial semicircle for **W** may be omitted from outlines, and phrases containing the words **week** and **were** may be formed:

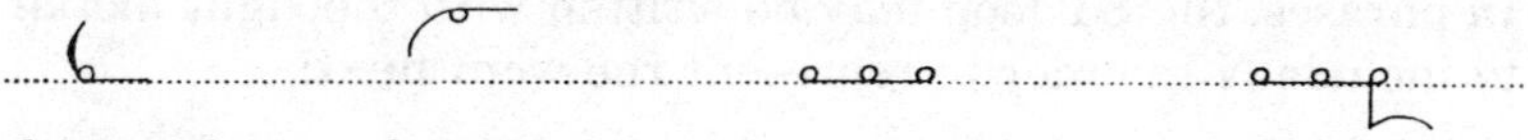

this week last week six weeks six weeks' time

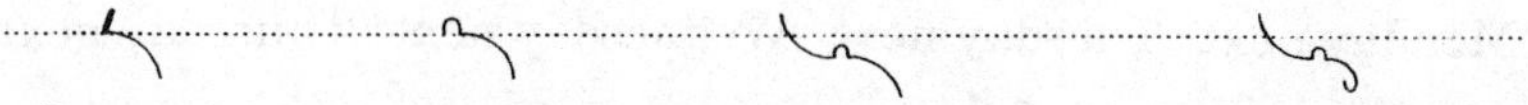

who were you were if you were if you were not

In phrases, the circle **S** may be used instead of the **ST** loop when writing **next:**

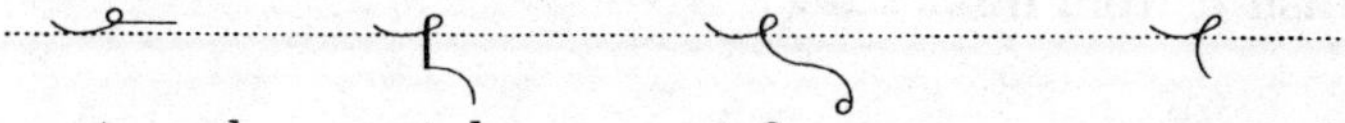

next week next door next few years next month

The stroke for **W** is used medially in phrases when a better joining results:

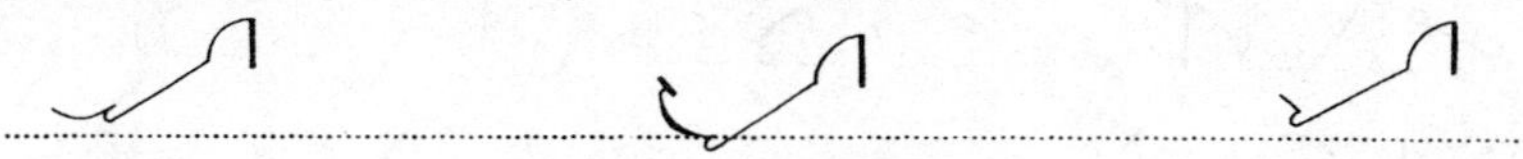

in the world all over the world of the world

throughout the world in this world in world trade

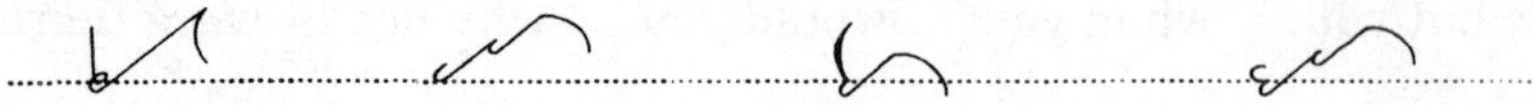

it is worth we were they were when we were

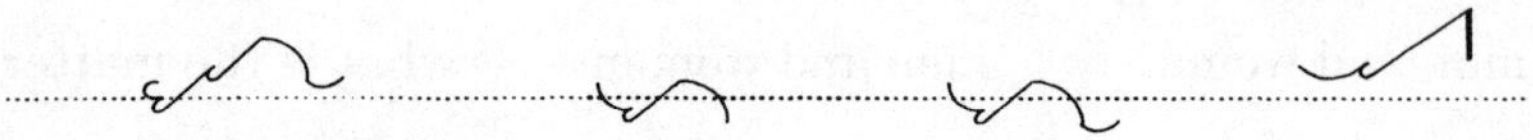

when we were not if it were if it were not in a word

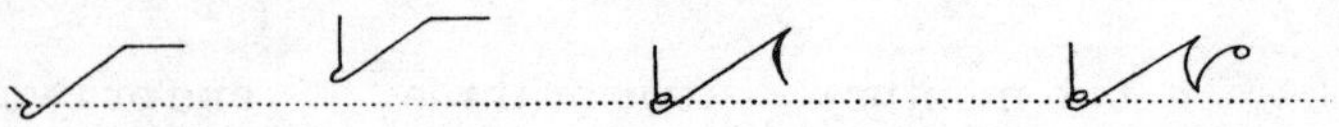

to work at work it is worthy it is worthless

Although the outline for the word **weeks** is often written by omitting the semicircle **W** in phrases, in a few cases stroke **W** gives a better joining than **K** and the **K** is omitted:

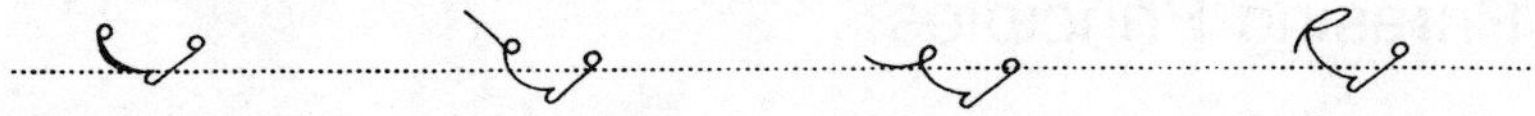

several weeks past few weeks next few weeks last few weeks

In phrases, the **ST** loop may be written with the right motion to include **N** in order to represent the word **next:**

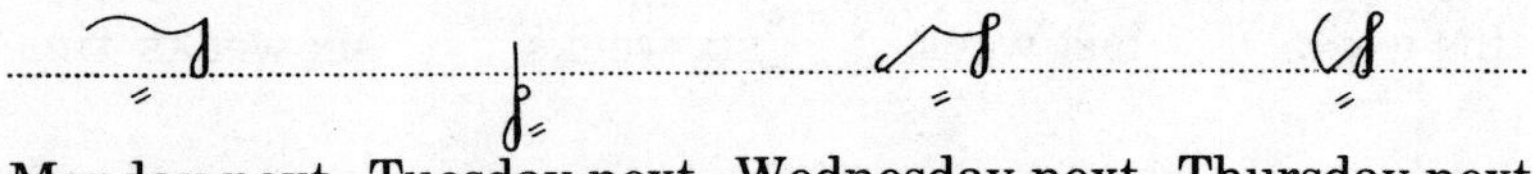

Monday next Tuesday next Wednesday next Thursday next

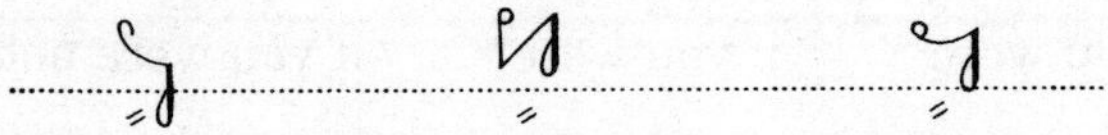

Friday next Saturday next Sunday next

Note: The outline for the word **newest** is written  to distinguish it from **next** .

Passage 1

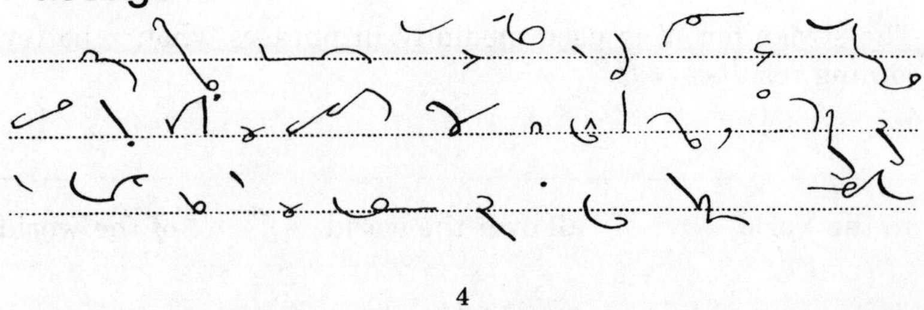

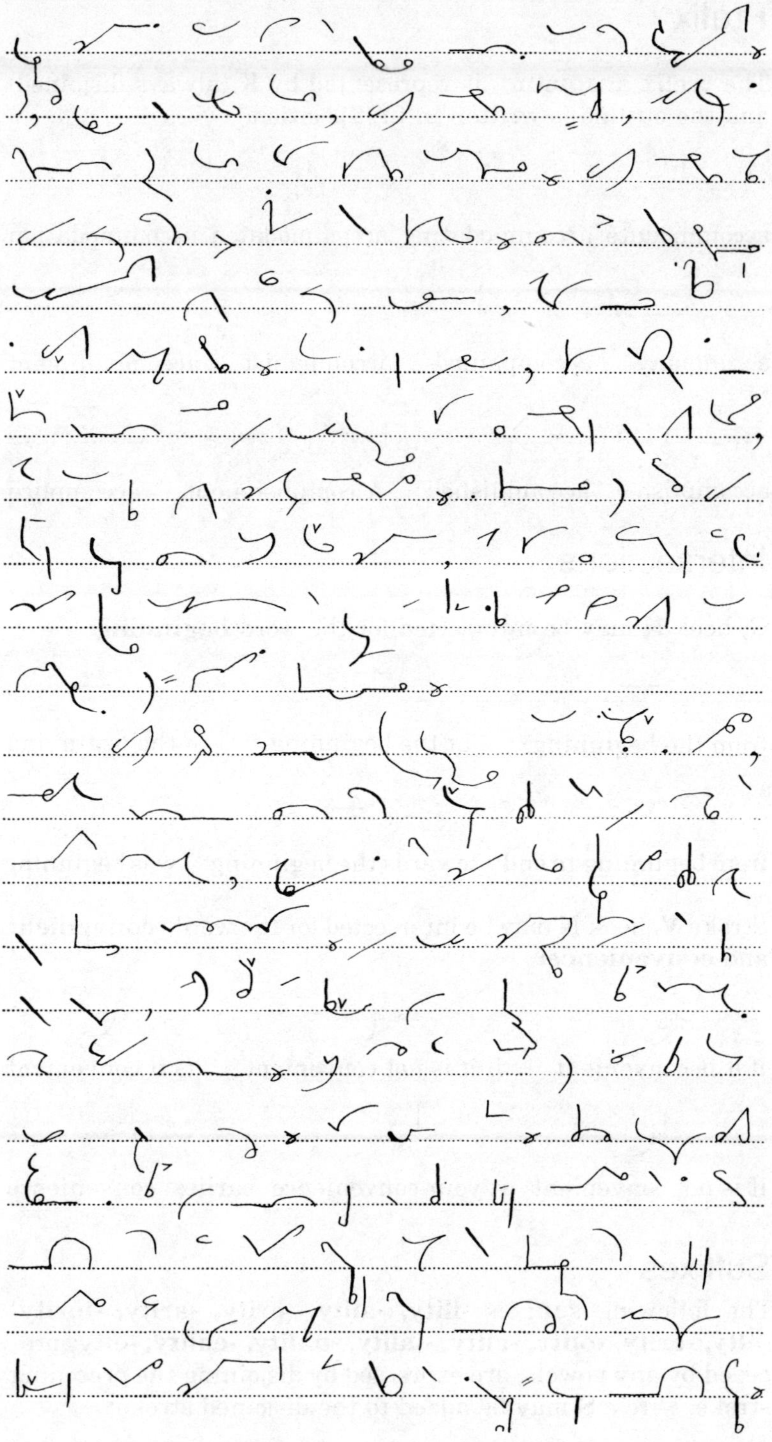

Prefix

The prefix **accom(m)-** is represented by **K** (always disjoined) and the outline is written in first position:

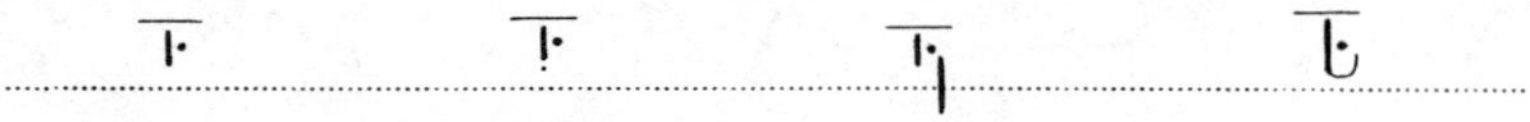

accommodate accommodating accommodated accommodation

accompany accompanied accompanist accompaniment

accomplish accomplished accomplishment accomplice

Intersections

G, hook **N** may be intersected for the word **beginning:**

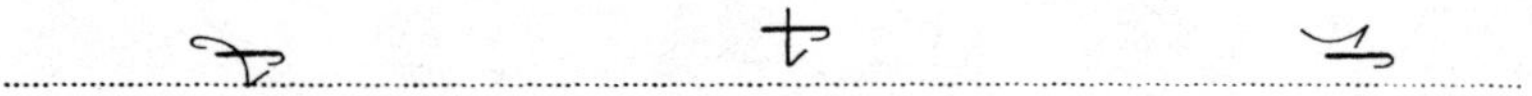

from the beginning at the beginning in the beginning

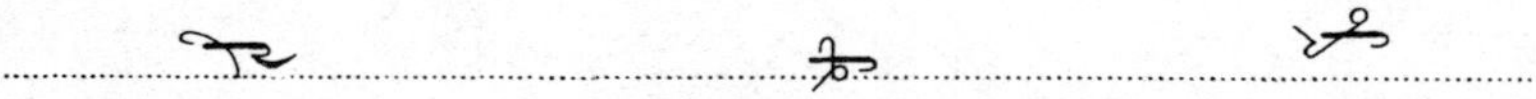

from beginning to end towards the beginning I was beginning

Stroke **V,** hook **N** may be intersected for the words **convenient** and **convenience:**

if it is convenient if it is not convenient is it convenient

it is not convenient at your convenience earliest convenience

Suffixes

The following suffixes **-ility, -ality, -ority, -arity, -iority, -alty, -erity, -olity, -elity, -iality, -uality, -eality, -elty,** preceded by any vowels, are expressed by disjoining the preceding stroke. Circle **S** may be added to the disjoined stroke:

solidarity legality novelty hospitality

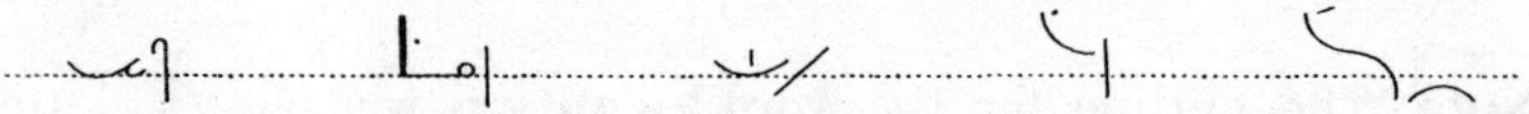

neutrality dexterity unreality fatality formality

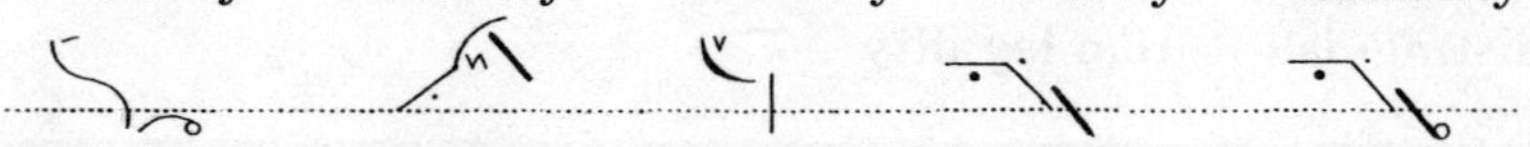

formalities reliability vitality capability capabilities

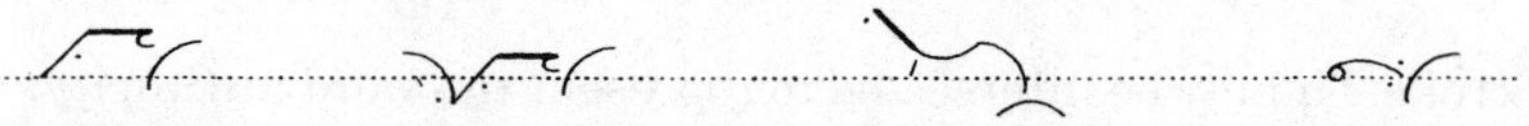

regularity irregularity abnormality similarity

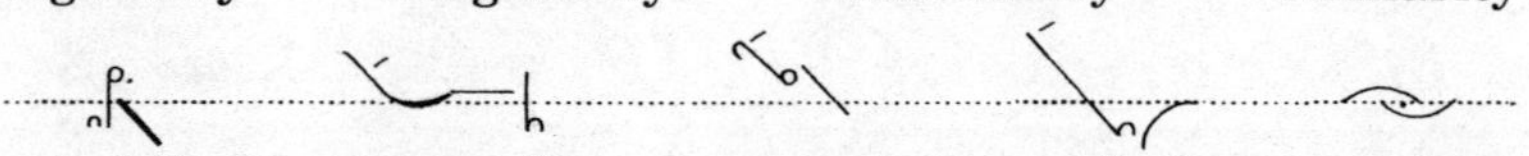

suitability punctuality prosperity popularity minority

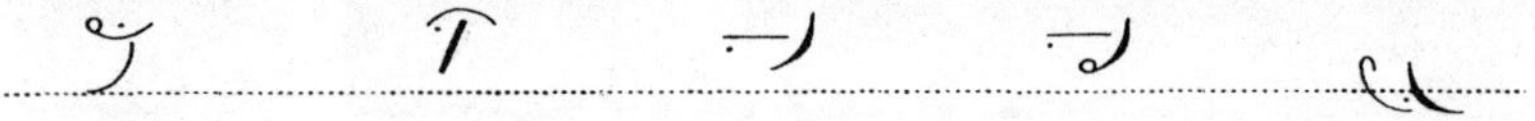

sensuality majority casualty casualties frivolity

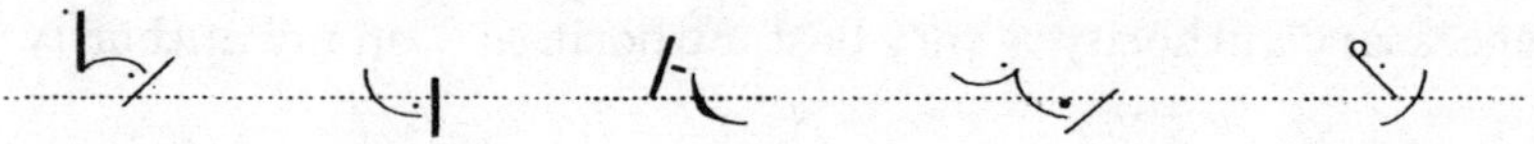

admiralty fidelity joviality inferiority speciality

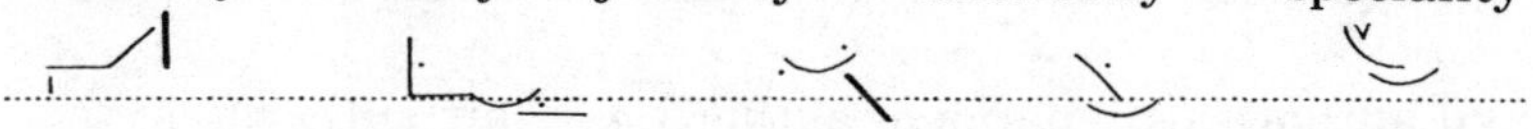

cordiality technicality inability penalty finality

A final circle or hook, or a half-length or double-length stroke may be used although a vowel immediately precedes the disjoined stroke, in which case the vowel is omitted:

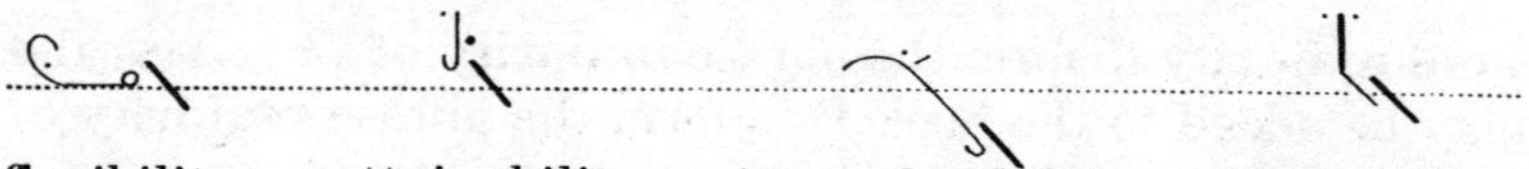

flexibility attainability imponderability adaptability

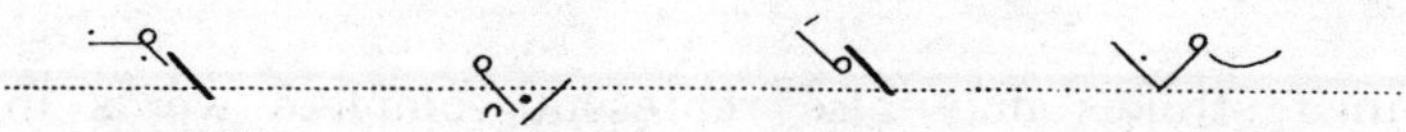

acceptability superiority possibility personality

When there is no stroke to disjoin, or the suffix follows the **shun hook,** the outline is written in full:

ability charity authority reality sincerity

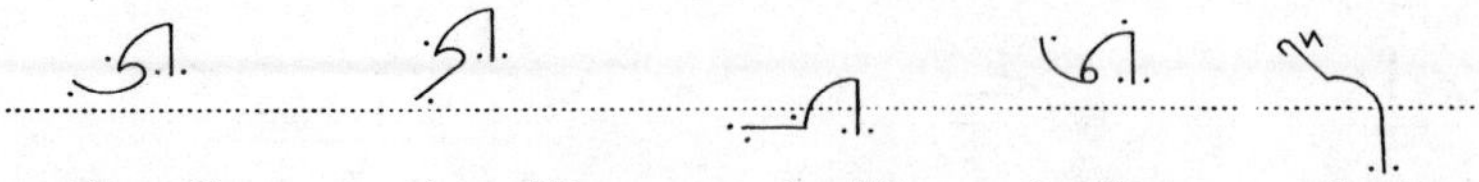

nationality rationality comicality facility priority

Note: The outline for the word **locality** is written 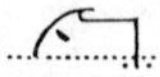 to distinguish it from **legality** .

Intersection

Stroke **Th** may be intersected to represent the word **authority:**

local authority higher authority several authorities

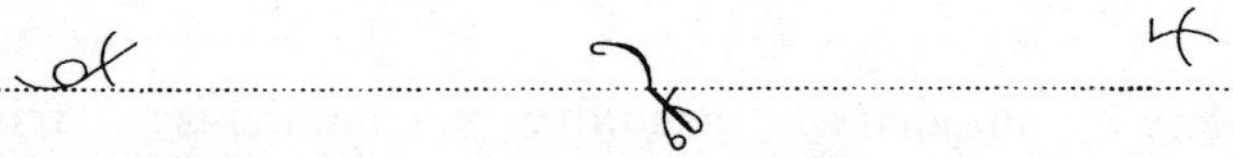

necessary authority very best authorities on my authority

civil authorities national authorities air authorities

Phrasing Principles

Hook **F** may be added to the disjoined **J** in the outline for the word **majority** to form the phrase **majority of** . Tick **the** may be added to the hook **F** to form the phrase **majority of the** .

Disjoined strokes may also represent complete words in phrases, and circle **S** may be added to the disjoined strokes:

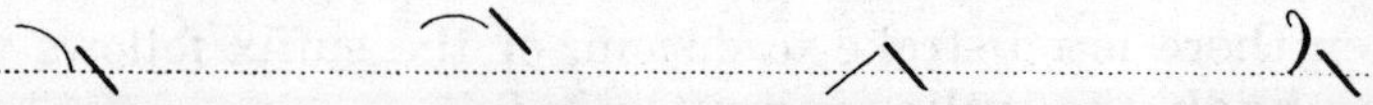

your ability my ability our ability their ability

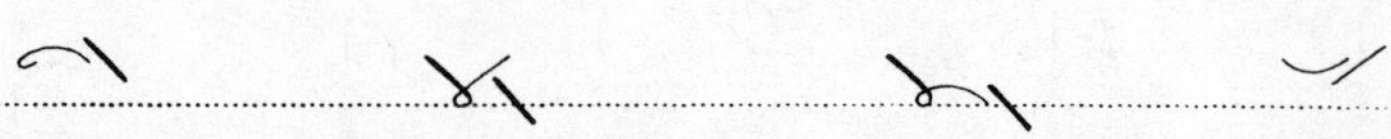

more ability best of our ability best of my ability in reality

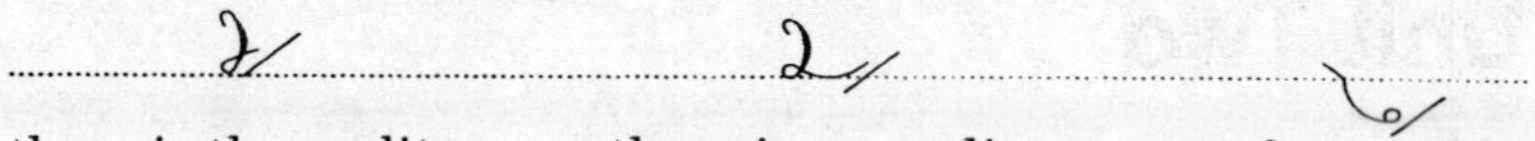

there is the reality there is no reality to face reality

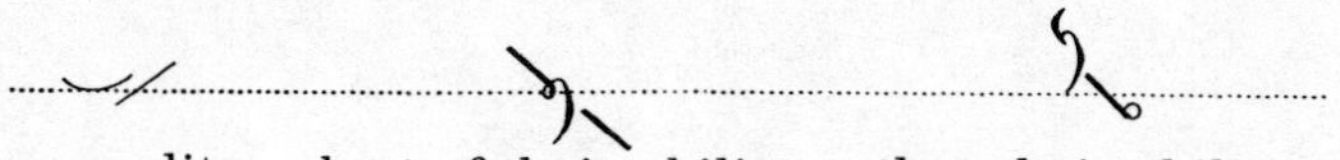

no reality best of their ability that their abilities

Passage 2

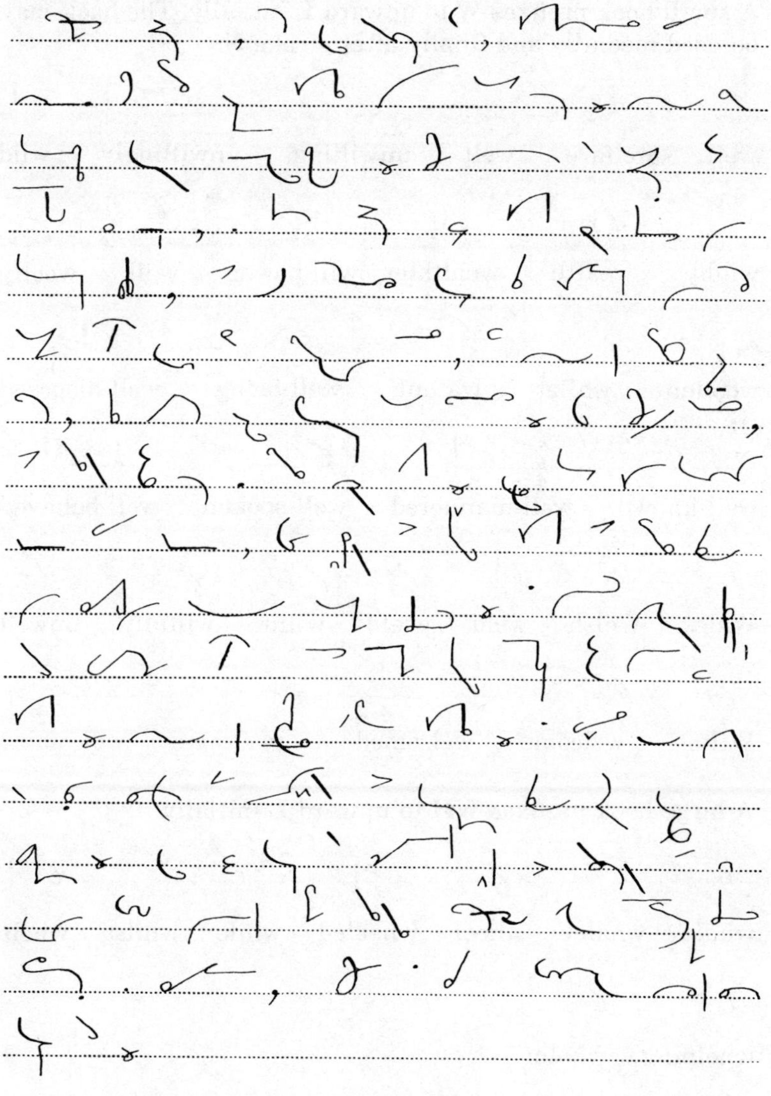

Unit Two

WL and WHL

A small hook prefixes **W** to upward **L** initially. The hook may be used medially and finally after stroke **N:**

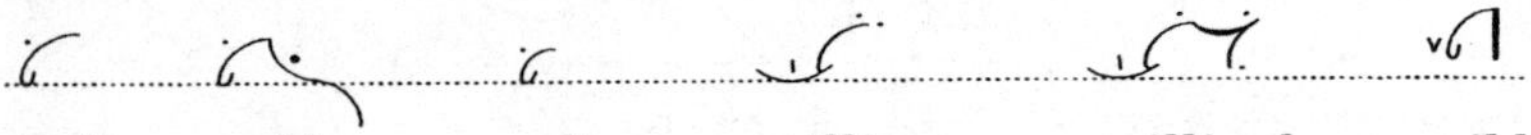

well welfare welt unwilling unwillingly wild

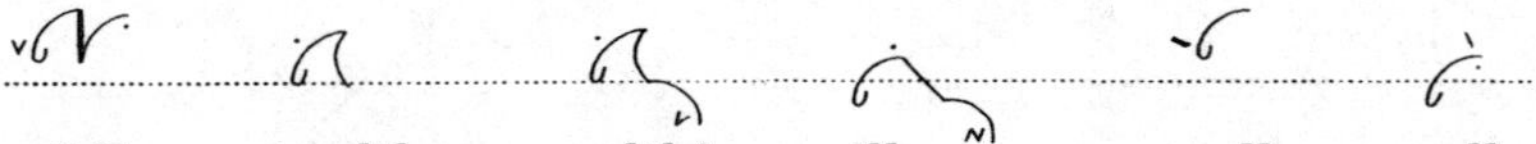

wildly wealth wealthier will-power wall woolly

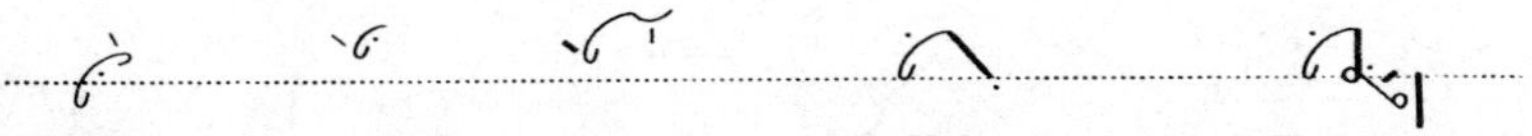

woollen wallet walnut well-being well-disposed

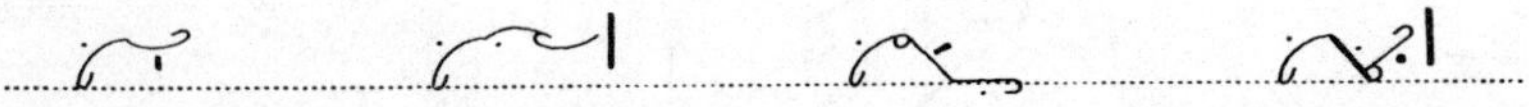

well-known well-mannered well-spoken well-behaved

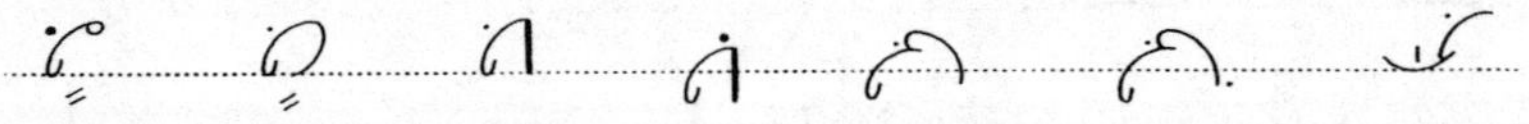

Wales Welsh weld wield wilful wilfully unwell

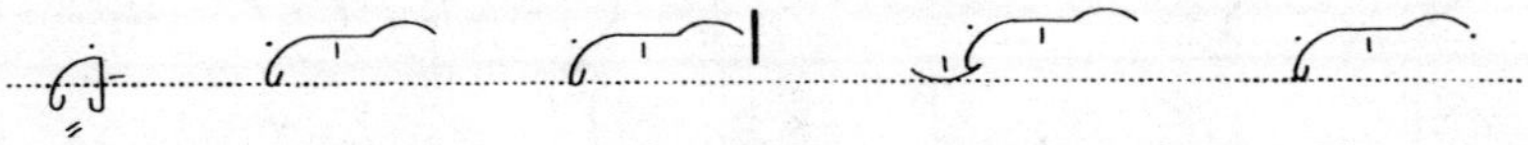

Wilton welcome welcomed unwelcome welcoming

A large hook prefixes **WH** to upward **L** initially:

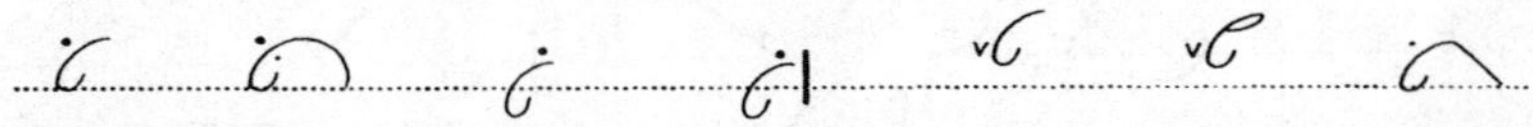

whale whaler wheel wheeled while whilst whelp

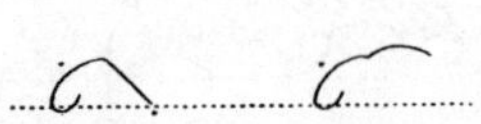

whelping whelm

The same **WH** hook may also be used medially and finally:

overwhelm meanwhile spinning-wheel

When **WH** is preceded by a vowel, the compound consonant for **WH** must be used:

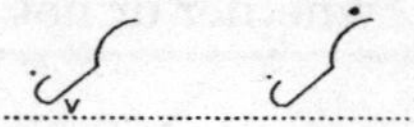

awhile awheel

Note: The outline for the word **pure** is written  to distinguish it from **poor**  , and the outline for the word **purest** is written  to distinguish it from **poorest** 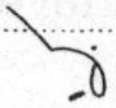 .

Short Forms and Derivatives

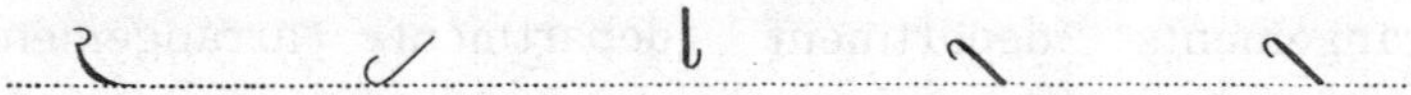

whatever whether advantage member remember

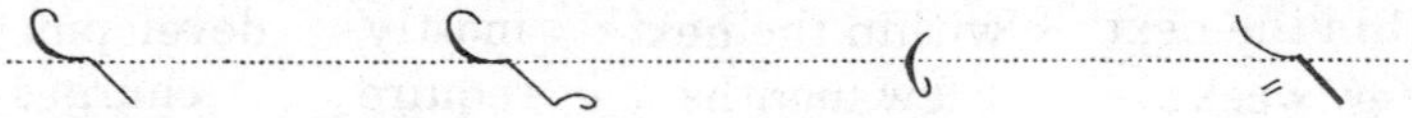

develop development within February

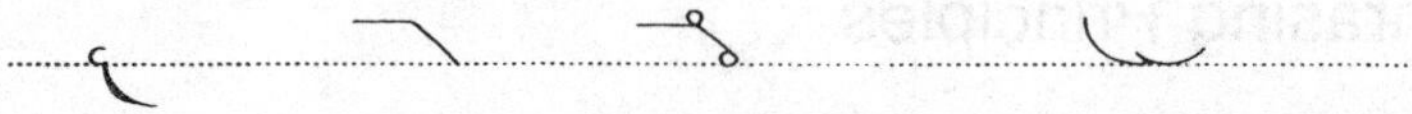

whenever capable expensive financial/financially

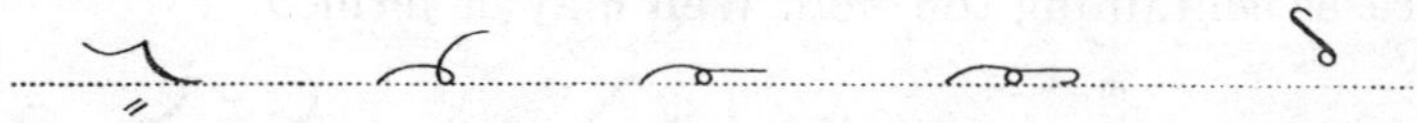

November mostly mistake mistaken balance

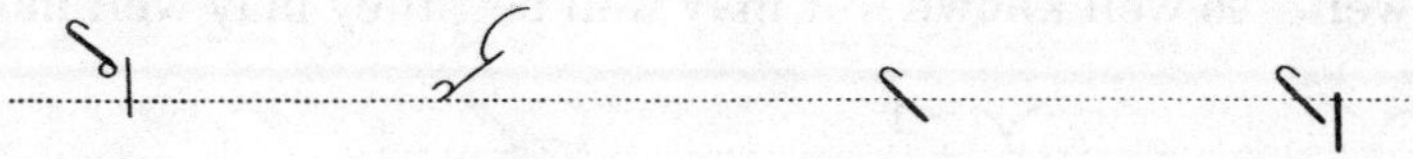

balanced worthwhile belief/believe believed

Phrases

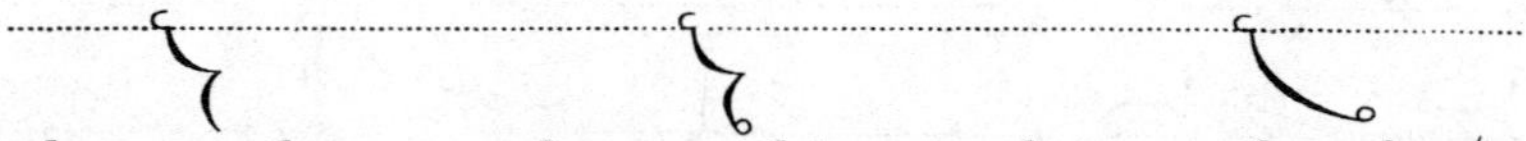

whenever they whenever this whenever there has/is

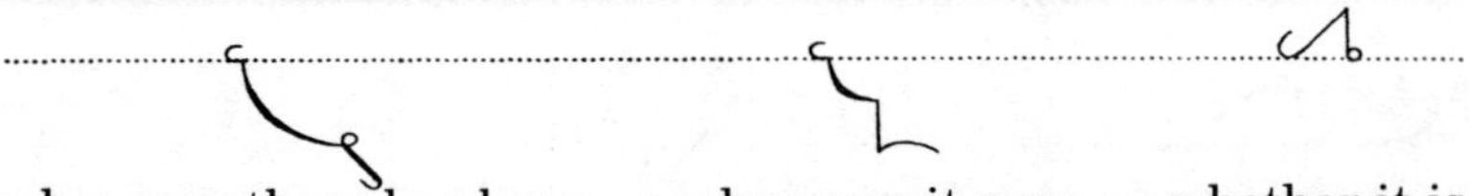

whenever there has been | whenever it may | whether it is

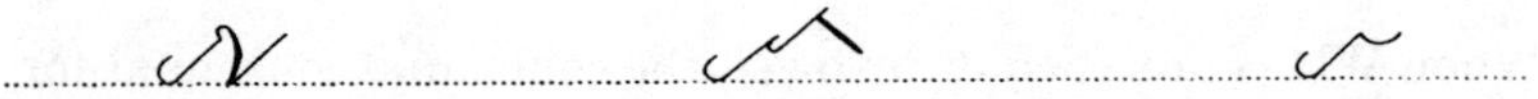

whether there are | whether we believe | whether or not

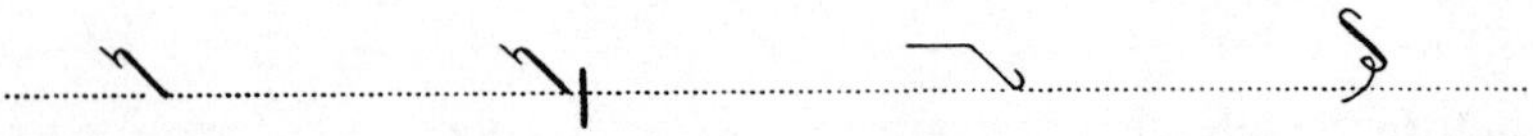

I remember | I remembered | capable of | balance sheet

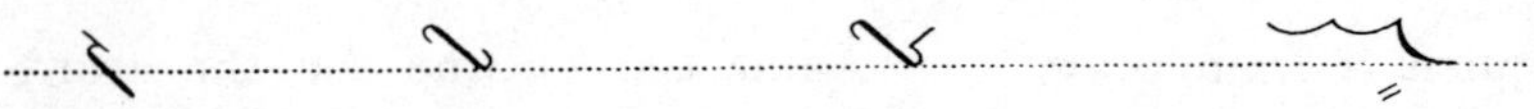

I believe | member of | member of the | in November

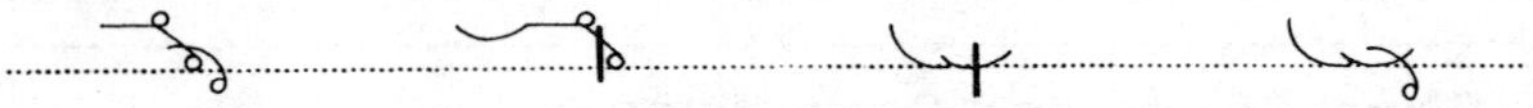

expensive arrangements | inexpensive department | financial department | financial arrangements

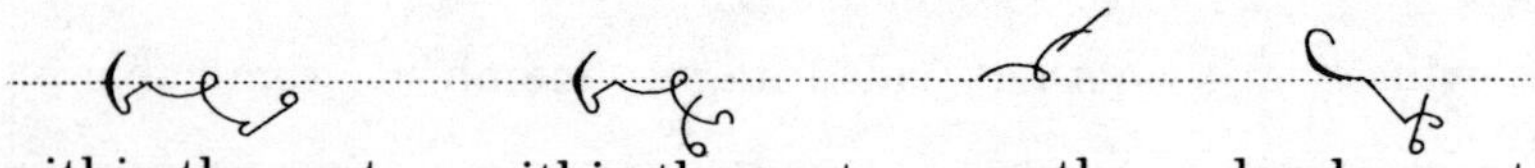

within the next few weeks | within the next few months | mostly require | development charges

Phrasing Principles

The initial hook for **W** may be omitted from outlines, and phrases containing the word **well** may be formed:

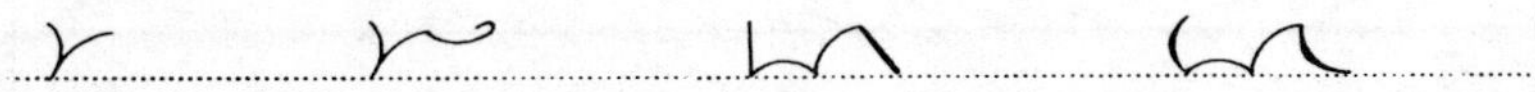

so well | so well known | it may well be | they may well have

very well | very well indeed | as it may well

Passage 3

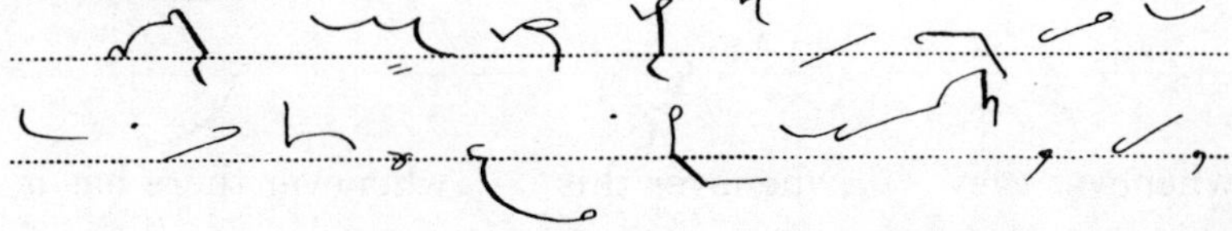

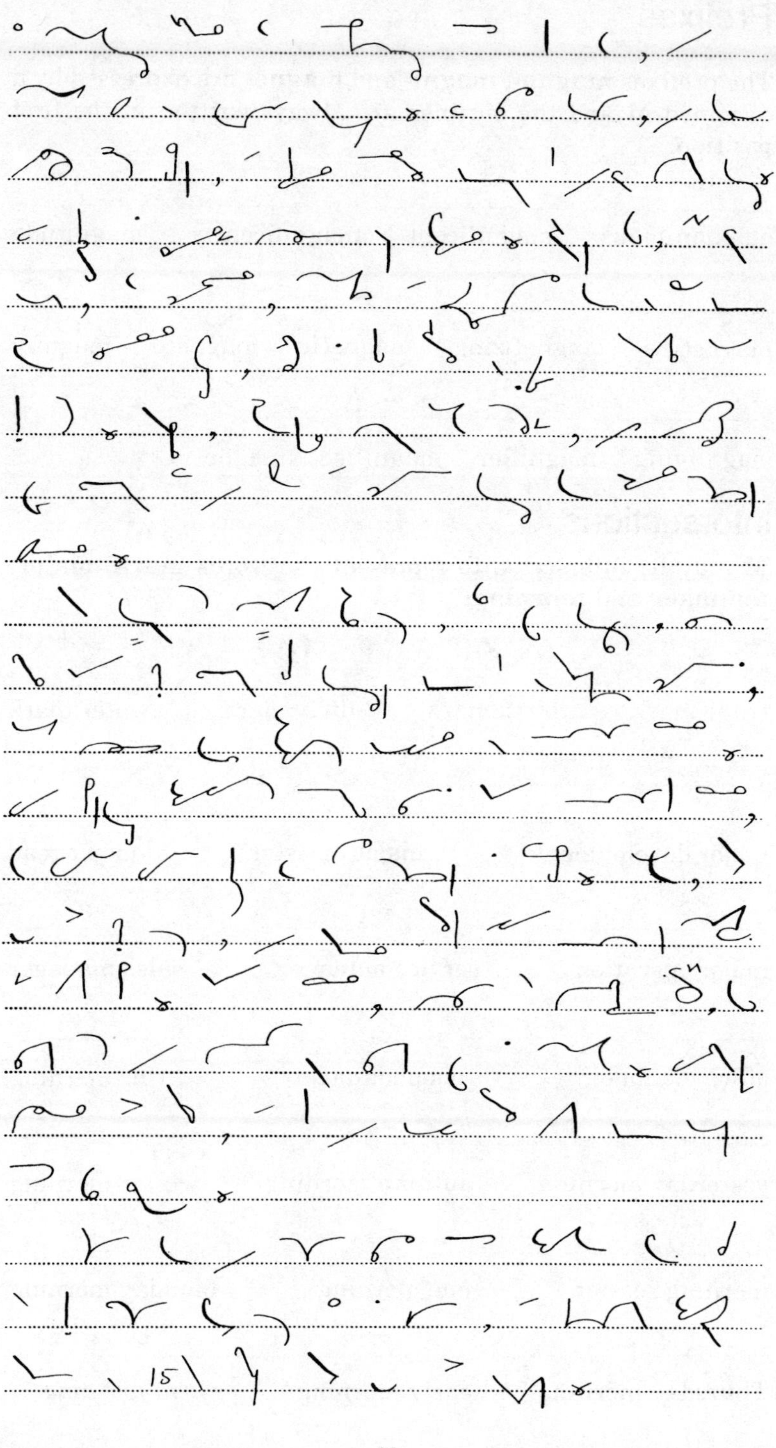

Prefixes

The prefixes **magna-, magni-** and **magne-** are expressed by a disjoined **M** and the outlines are always written in the first position:

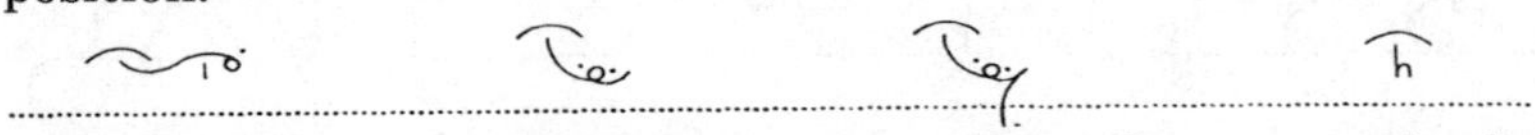

magnanimous   magnificent   magnificently   magnitude

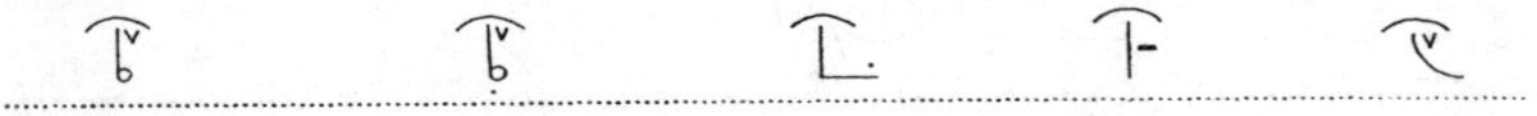

magnetize   magnetizing   magnetic   magneto   magnify

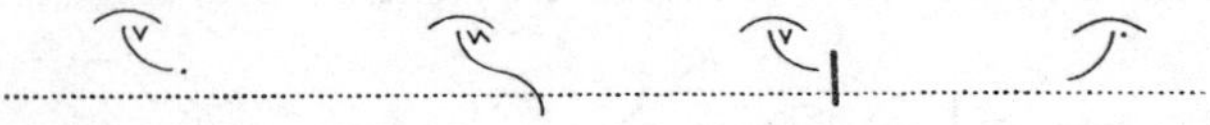

magnifying   magnifier   magnified   magnesia

Intersections

M may be intersected to represent the words **mark, major, manager** and **morning:**

trade mark   birth mark   dirty mark   water mark

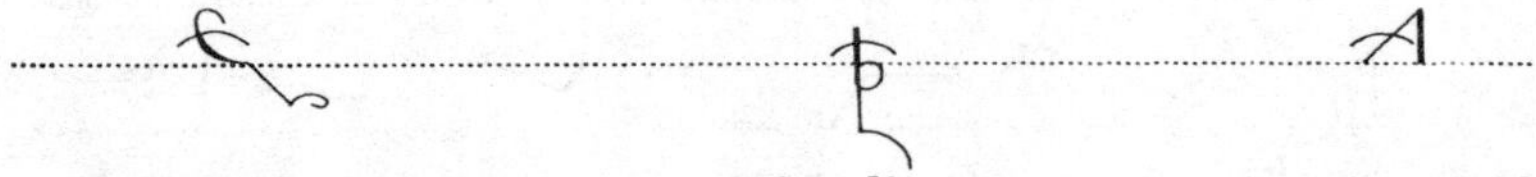

major development   major disaster   major road

major operation   service manager   sales manager

office manager   shop manager   this morning

yesterday morning   autumn morning   winter morning

morning session   one morning   Monday morning

Thursday morning   early morning   warm morning

Suffixes

The suffixes **-logical** and **-logically** are represented by a disjoined **J**:

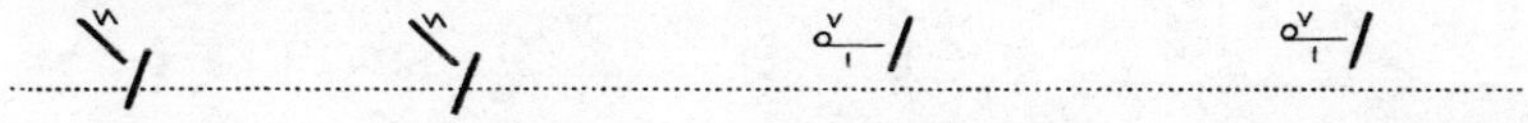

biological biologically psychological psychologically

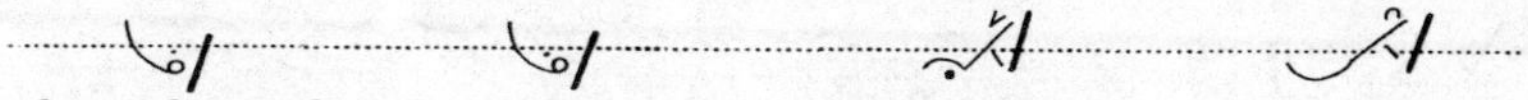

physiological physiologically meteorological neurological

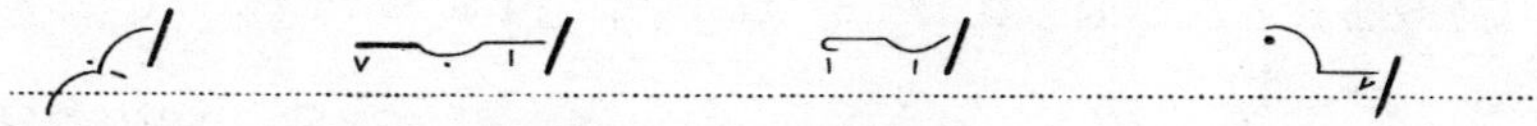

illogical gynaecological chronological archaeological

Phrasing Principles

A disjoined **J** may be written to represent the word **logical** in phrases:

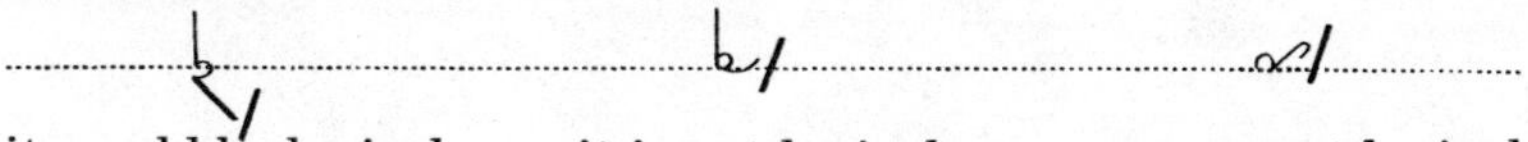

it would be logical it is not logical you are not logical

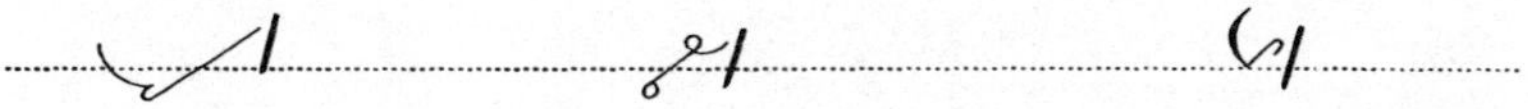

if we are logical he is not logical they are not logical

Passage 4

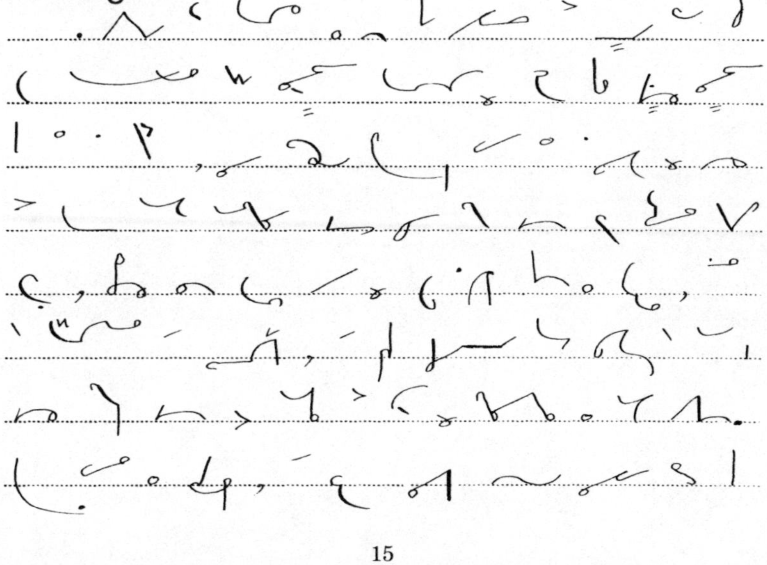

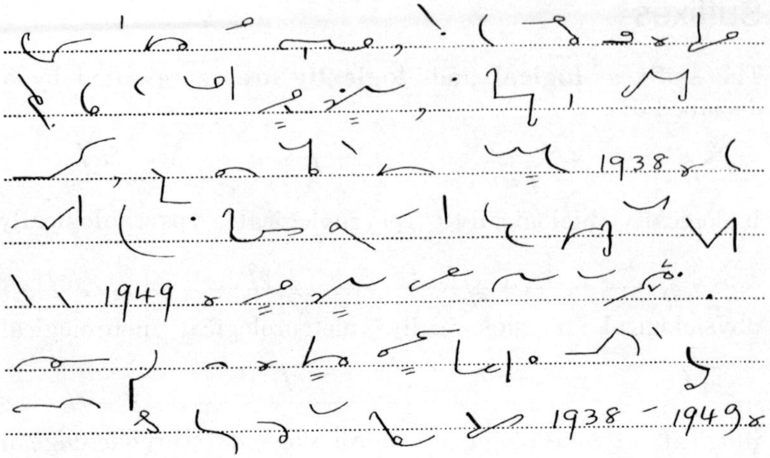
1938
1949
1938 - 1949

Unit Three

SW circle

A large initial circle represents the sound **SW**. Circle **SW** is written in the same direction as circle **S**:

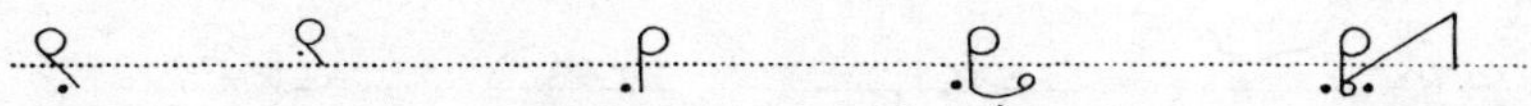

sweep swept sweet/suite sweetness sweetheart

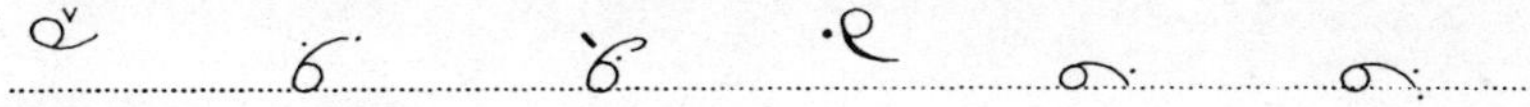

swine swelling swollen suave swim swimming

swimmingly swerve swerving suede swear swift

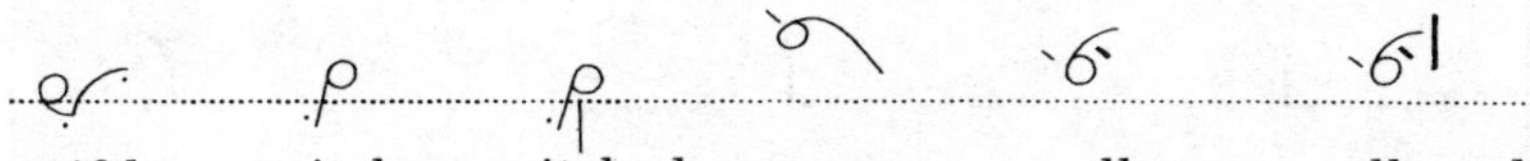

swiftly switch switched swamp swallow swallowed

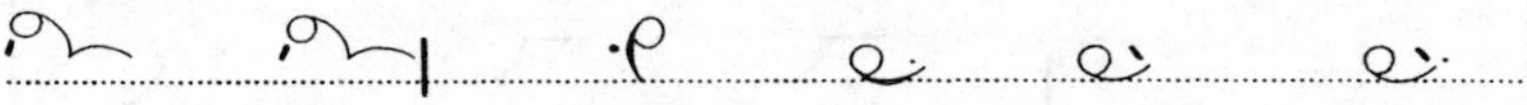

swarm swarmed swathe swing swoon swooning

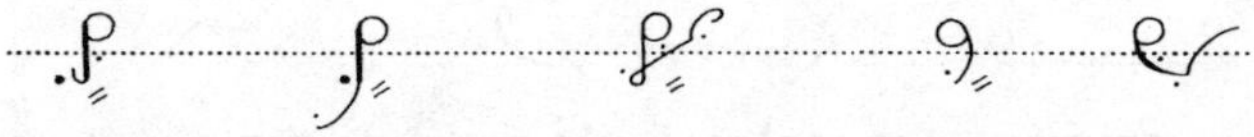

Sweden Swedish Switzerland Swiss swivel

The large circle **SW** is written on the hook **R** side of straight strokes to include **R**:

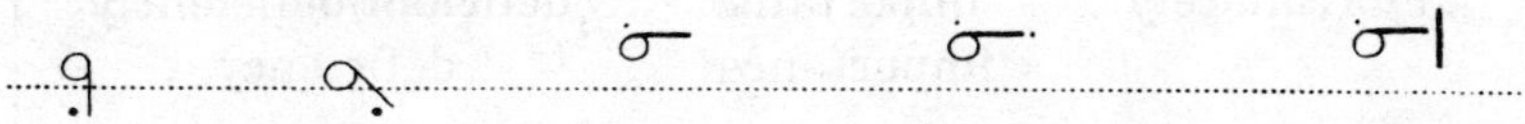

sweeter sweeper swagger swaggering swaggered

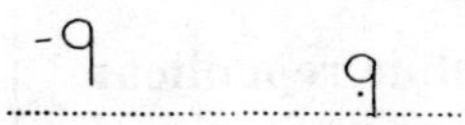

swatter sweater

When **S** and **W** are the only consonants in a word, and in derivatives, circle **S** and stroke **W** must be used:

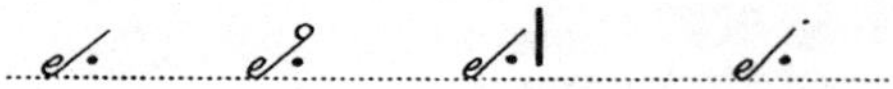

sway sways swayed swaying

The circle **SW** is not used in the middle of an outline:

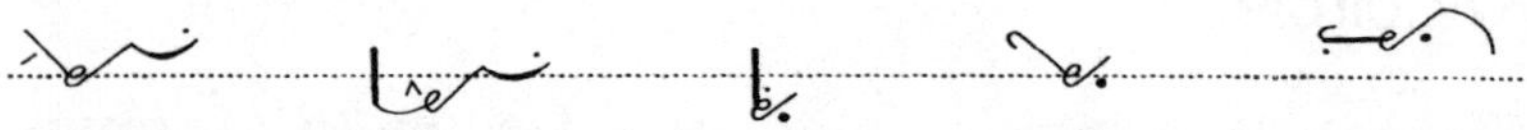

upswing downswing dissuade persuade glassware

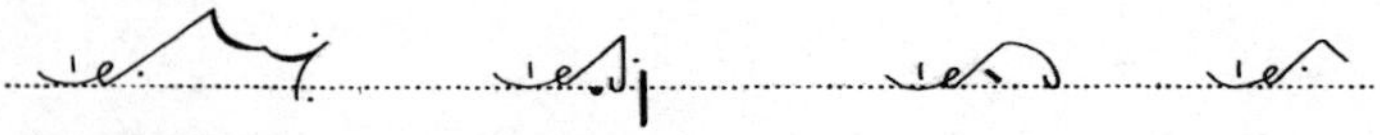

unswervingly unsweetened unsworn unswept

Short Forms and Derivatives

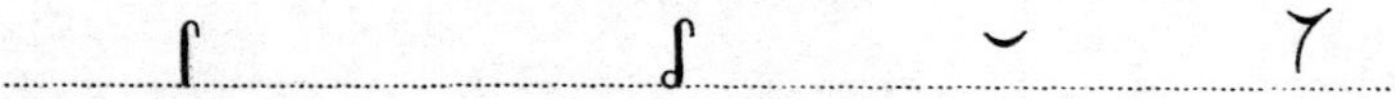

deliver/delivery deliverance hand handle

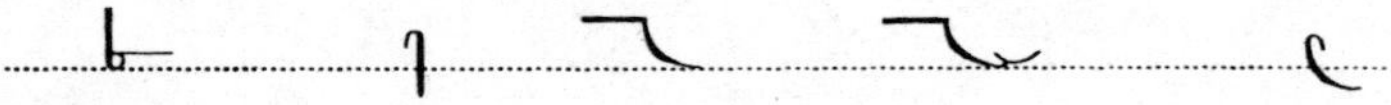

description during govern government however

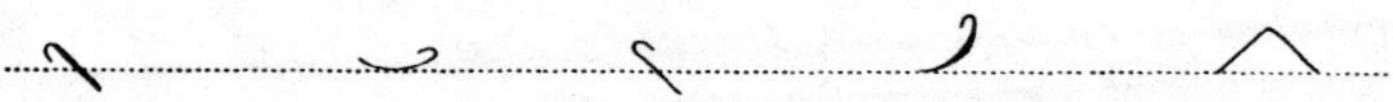

number opinion people pleasure represent

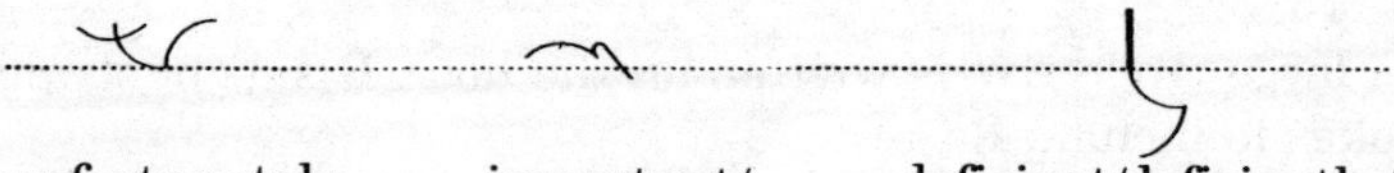

unfortunately important/importance deficient/deficiently/deficiency

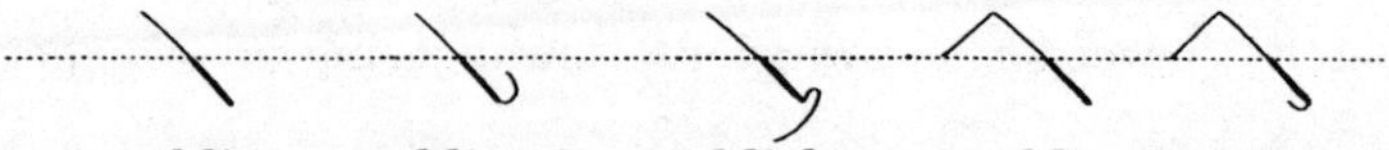

public/publicly publish publication publisher republic republican

Phrasing Principles

The circle **SW** may be used to represent the words **as we** in phrases:

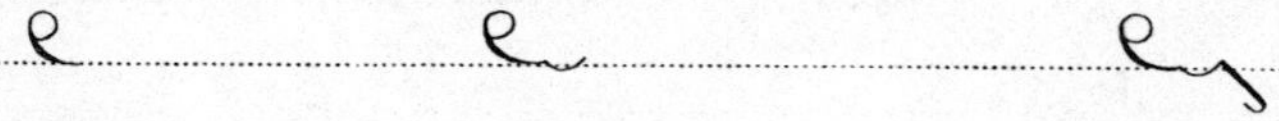

as we have as we have not as we have not been

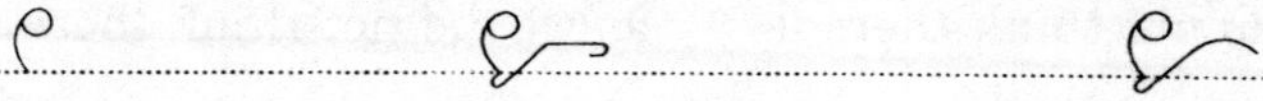

as we think as we think we can as we think we may

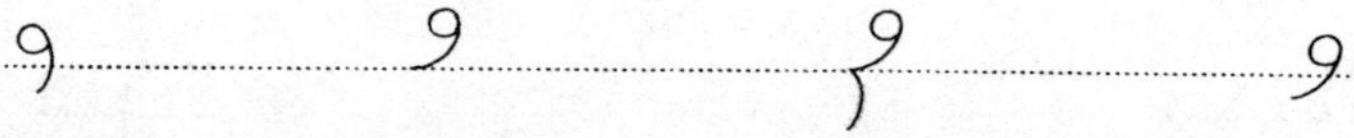

as we see as we shall as we shall see as we wish

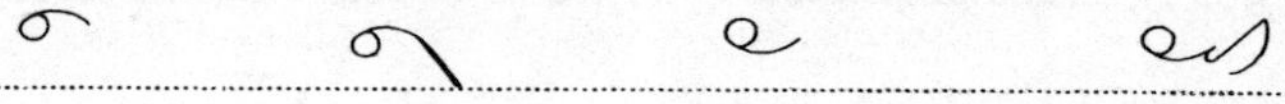

as we may as we may be as we know as we know we shall

as we can as we can see as we are as we feel as we felt

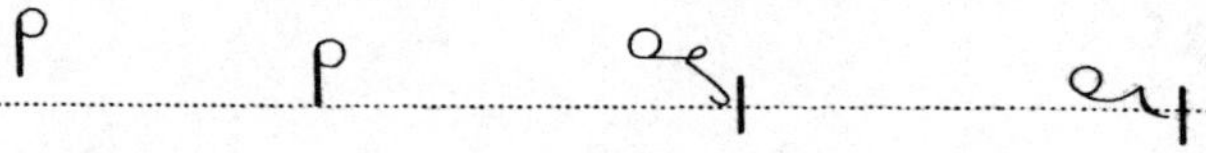

as we had as we do as we explained as we invited

The circle **SW** may be used to form the following phrases:

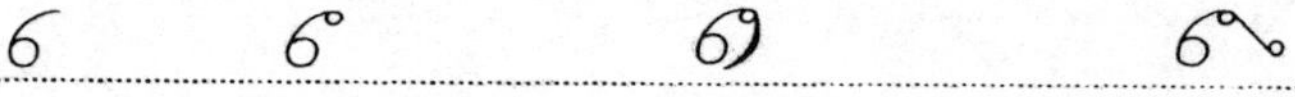

as well as well as as well as usual as well as possible

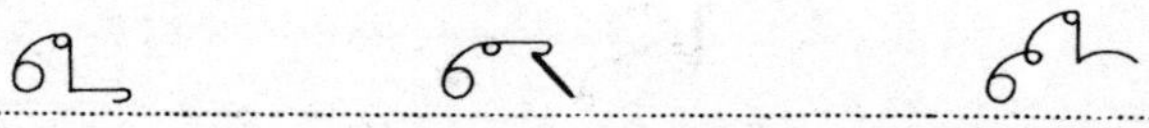

as well as it can as well as can be as well as last time

The circle **SW** may be written to a half-length and a double-length stroke:

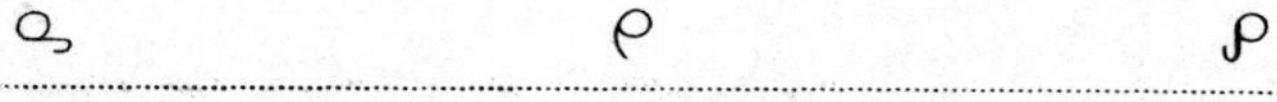

as we cannot as we thought as we had not

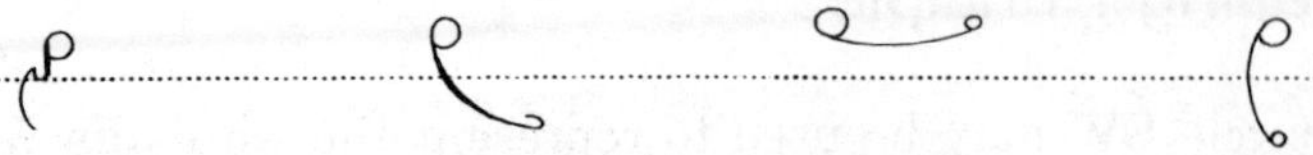

as we do not think — as we have been there — as we know there is — as we think there is

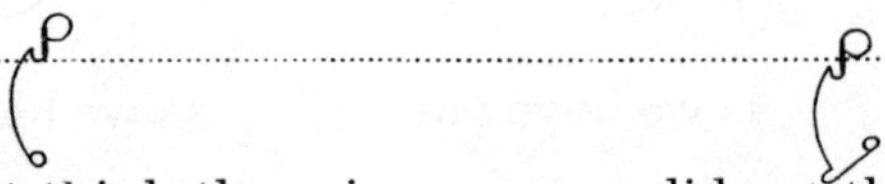

as we do not think there is — as we did not think there was

The large initial circle **SW** may also be combined with the hook **R** to straight strokes to form other phrases:

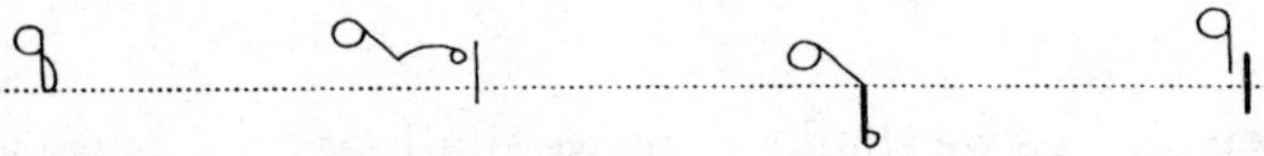

as we trust — as we promised — as we produce — as we tried

The initial circle **SW** may not be used in the phrases:

as we went — as we want

Phrases

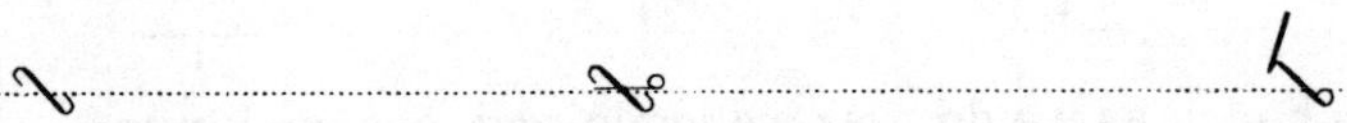

number of — number of companies — large numbers

large number of — large number of inquiries — during the

during the year — during the last few years — during the last few weeks

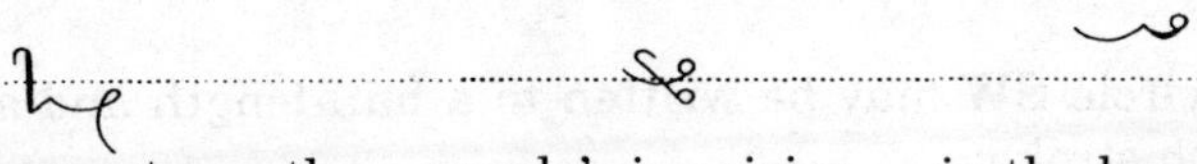

during the next month — people's inquiries — in the hands of

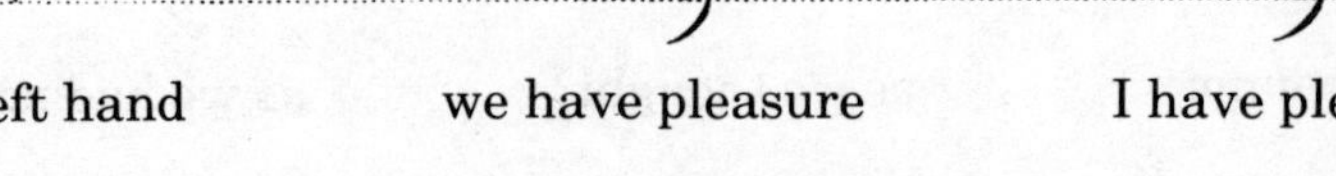

left hand — we have pleasure — I have pleasure

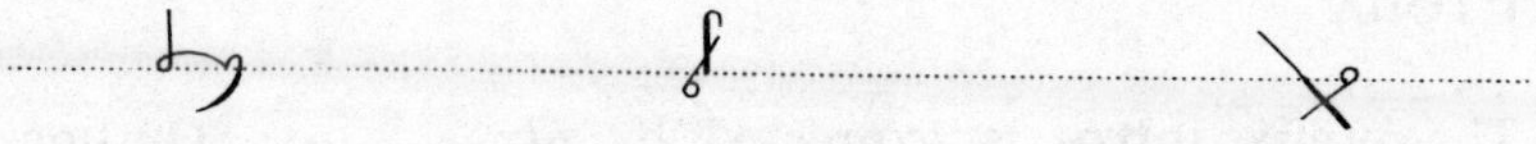

it is my pleasure delivery charges public requirements

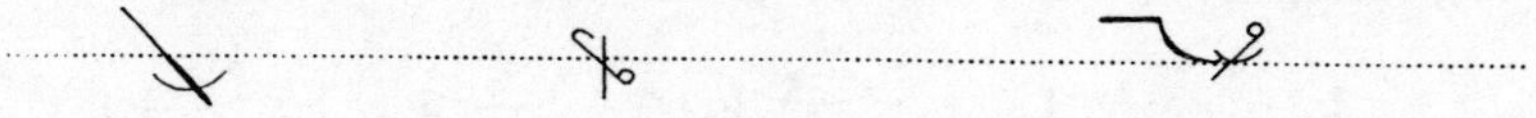

public inquiry people's attention government requirements

Note: A useful phrase is **on the other hand** , formed from **on the other** .

Passage 5

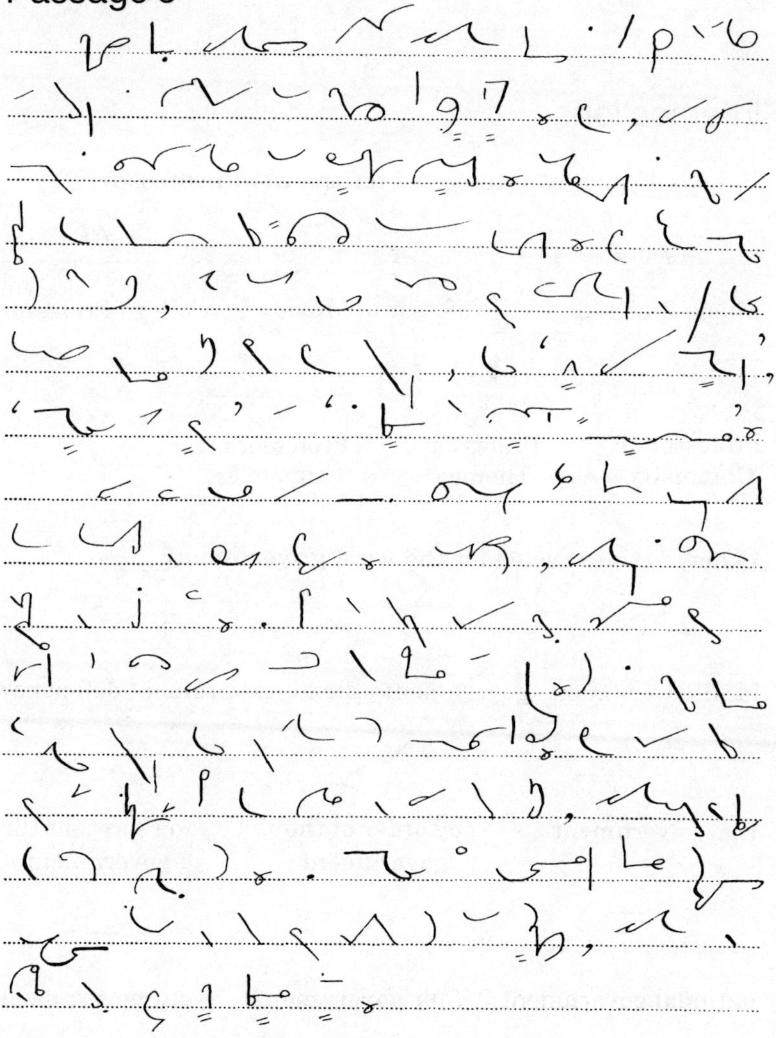

Prefix

The prefix **intro-** is expressed by **ntr** . Outlines beginning with **intro** are written in the third position:

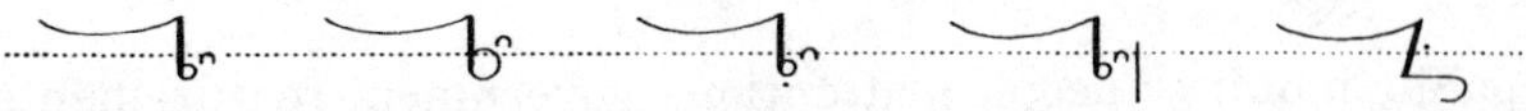

introduce introduces introducing introduced introjection

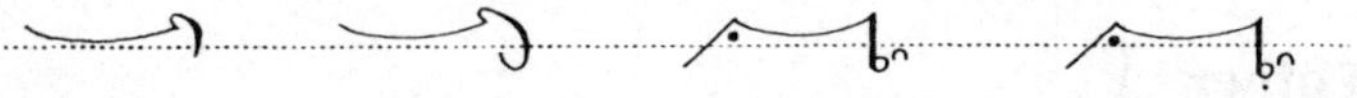

introvert introversion reintroduce reintroducing

Intersections

P, hook **R** may be intersected for the word **professor:**

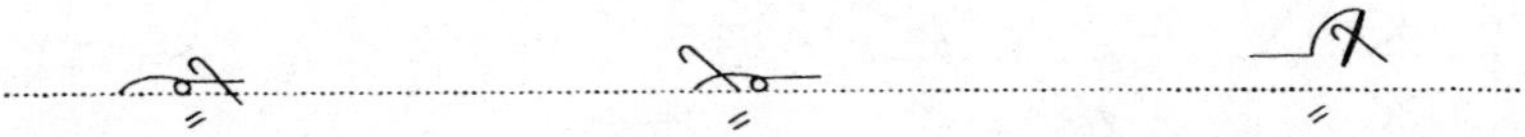

Music Professor Professor of Music College Professor

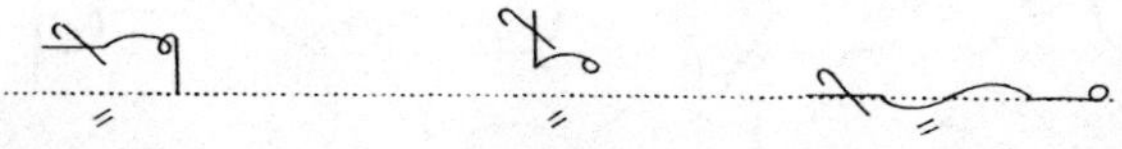

Professor of Chemistry Professor Thomas Professor of Economics

G may be intersected for the word **government**:

local government government official government deficiency

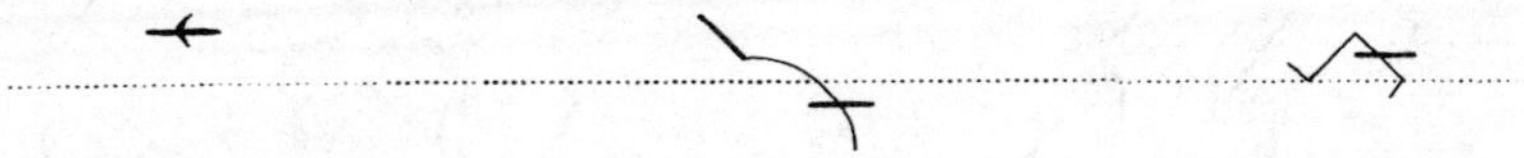

that government by order of the government to represent the government

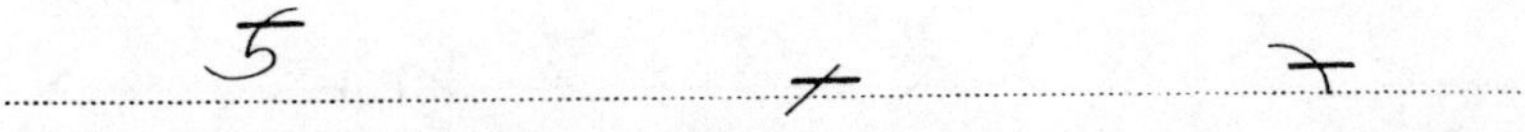

national government our government your government

their government other governments better government

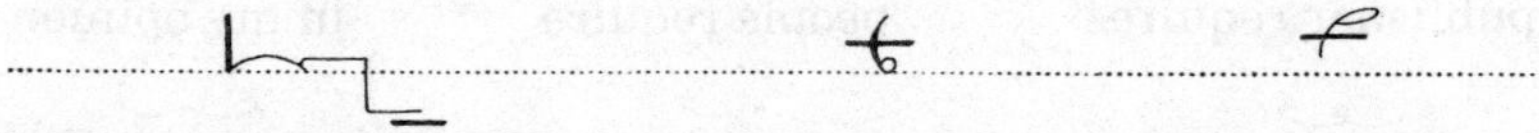

democratic government this government last government

Stroke **S** may be intersected for the words **society** and **scientific:**

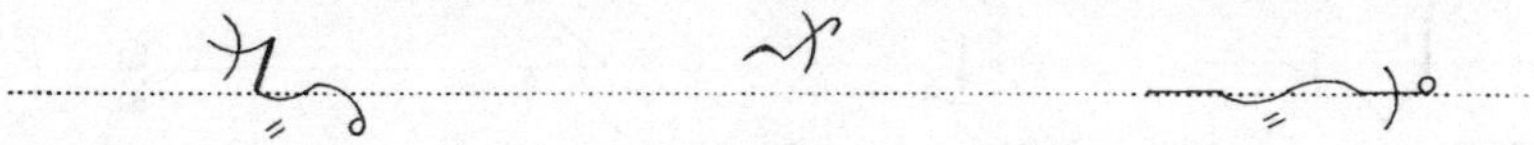

Society of Engineers modern society Economics Society

for their society scientific research scientific work

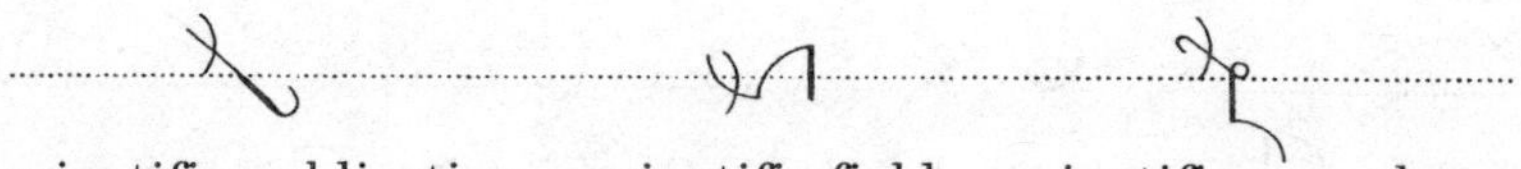

scientific publication scientific field scientific procedure

Suffixes

The suffixes **-mental, -mentally, -mentality** are expressed by a disjoined **mnt** :

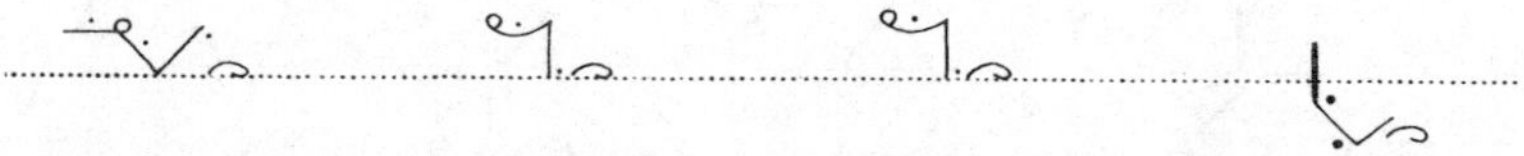

experimental sentimental sentimentality departmental

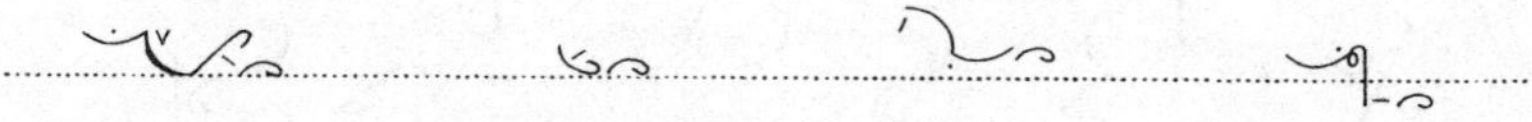

environmental fundamental ornamental instrumental

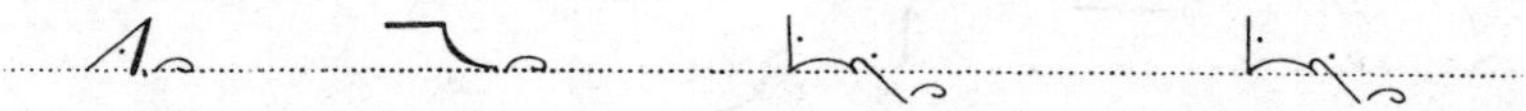

regimental governmental temperamental temperamentally

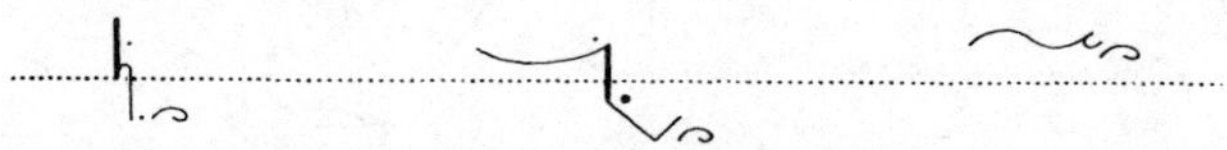

detrimental inter-departmental monumental

Phrases

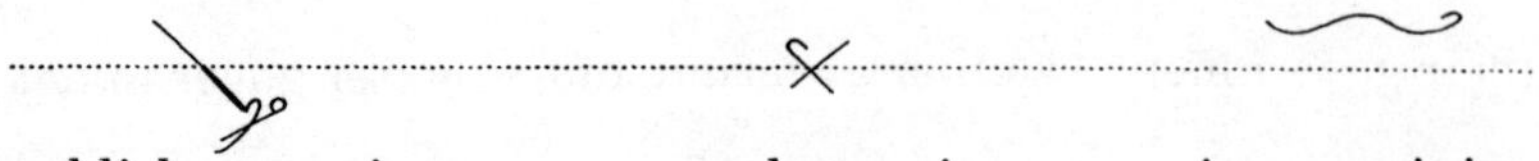

publisher requires | people require | in my opinion

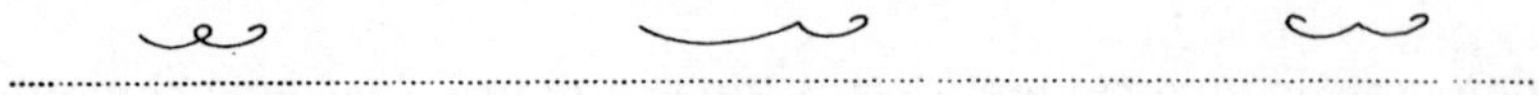

in his opinion | in their opinion | in our opinion

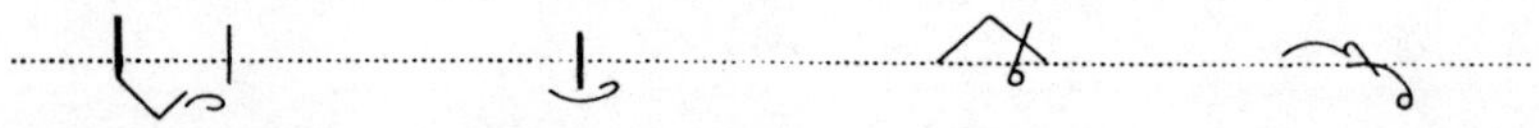

departmental committee | difference of opinion | represent charges | important arrangements

Passage 6

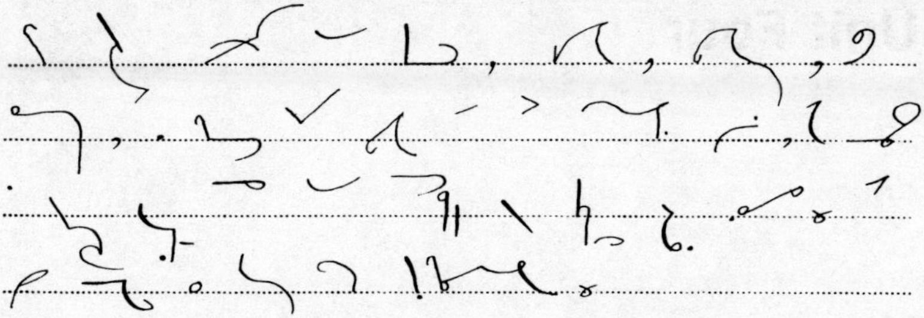

Unit Four

Prefix

The prefix **self-** is represented by a disjoined circle **S** written close to the following stroke. The outlines are written in second position as they take the position of the vowel in the prefix:

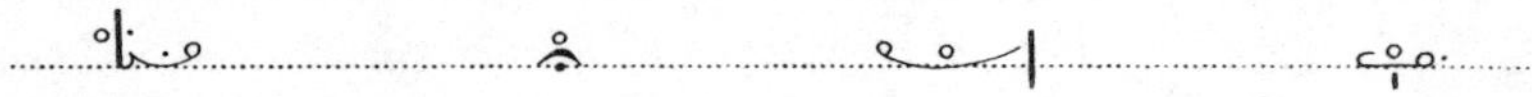

self-defence   self-made   self-centred   self-closing

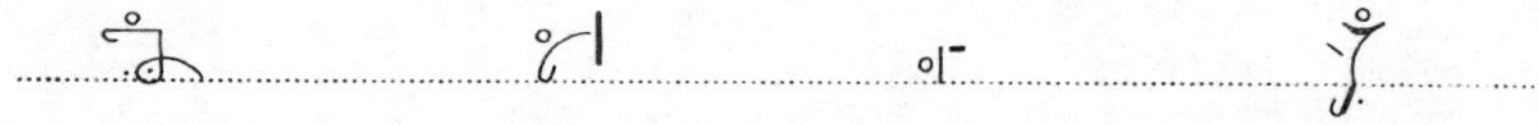

self-criticism   self-willed   self-taught   self-indulgent

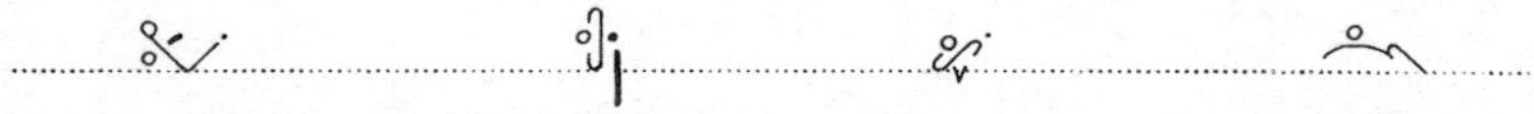

self-supporting   self-trained   self-winding   self-important

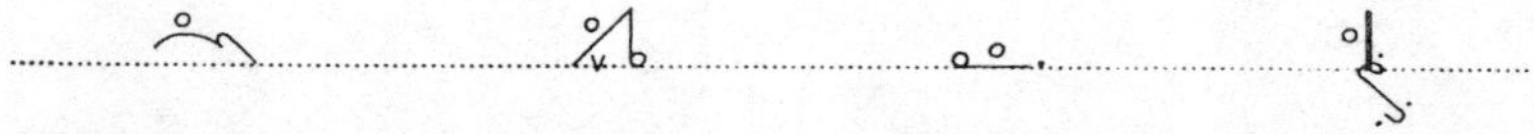

self-importance   self-righteous   self-seeking   self-discipline

self-dedication   self-improvement   self-help   self-denial

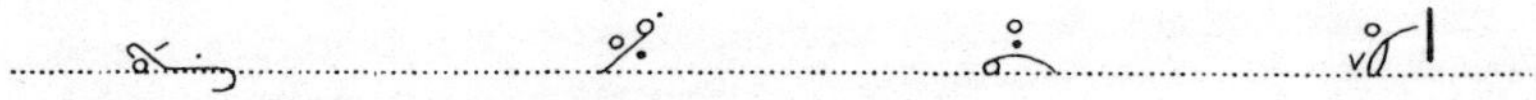

self-protection   self-raising   self-same   self-styled

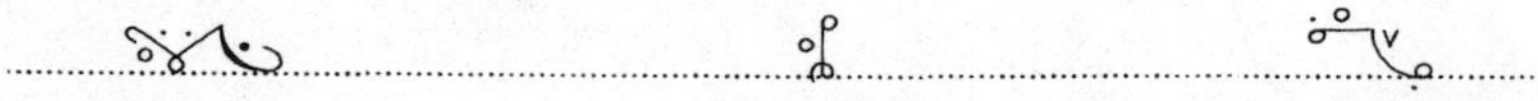

self-preservation   self-satisfaction   self-sacrifice

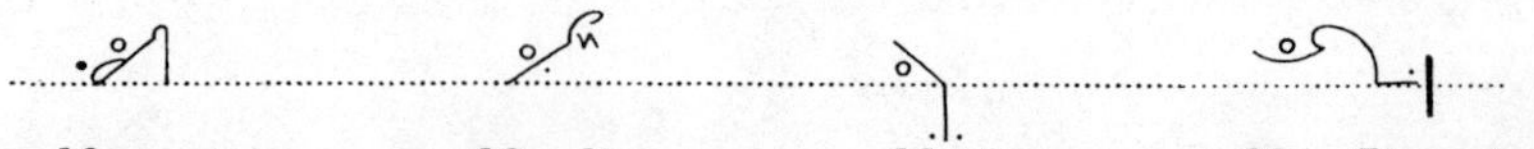

self-starter   self-reliant   self-pity   self-inflicted

Short Forms and Derivatives

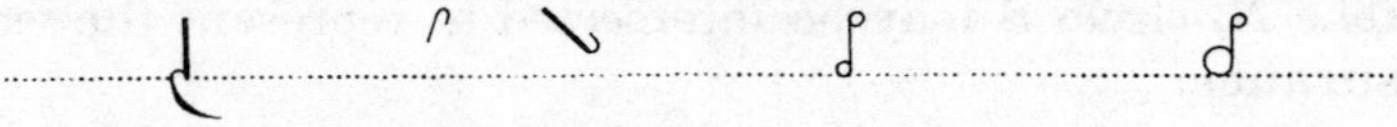

advertise/ advertisement | child | behalf | circumstance | circumstances

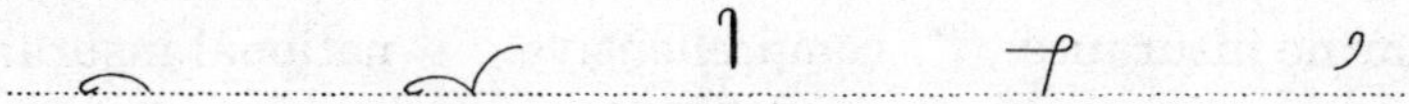

Mr./mere | merely | doctor/ Dr. | exchange | short

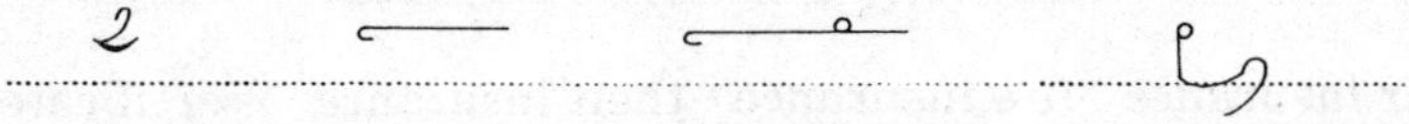

shorthand | character | characteristic | circumstantial

representative | unanimous/unanimously/unanimity

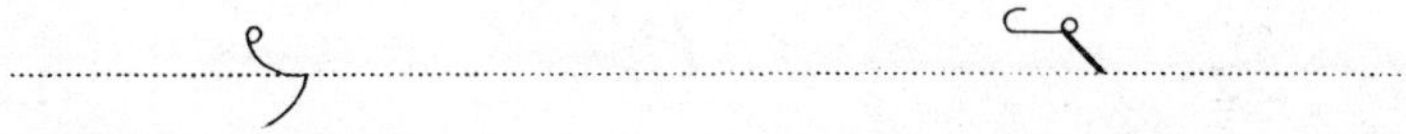

sufficient/sufficiently/ sufficiency | questionable/questionably

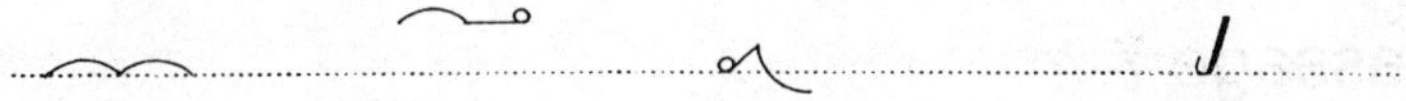

minimum | maximum | certificate | general/generally

insurance | investigation | introduction

Phrases

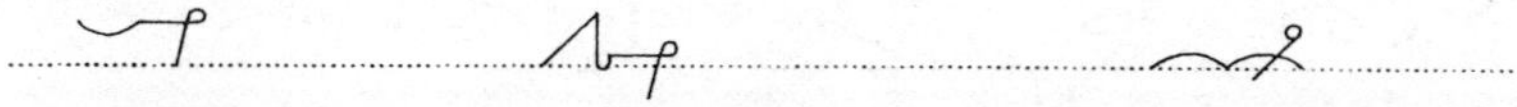

in exchange | rate of exchange | minimum requirements

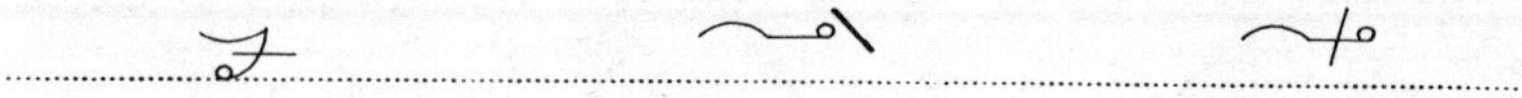

insurance company | maximum ability | maximum charge

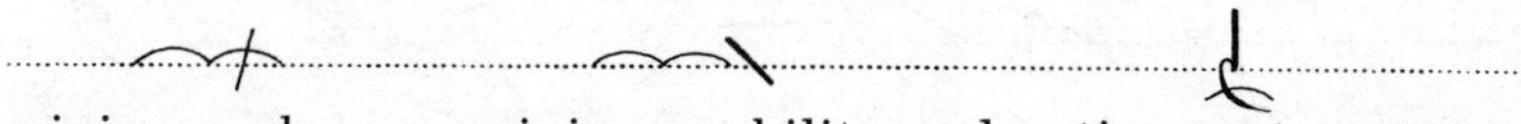

minimum charge | minimum ability | advertisement manager

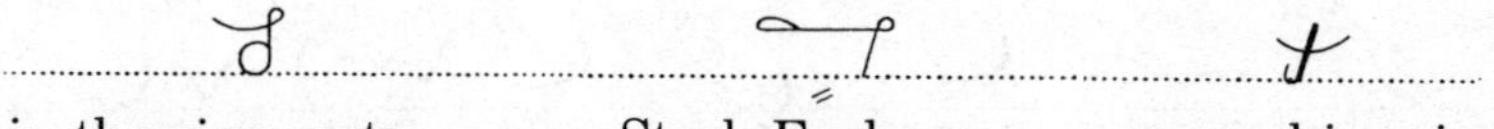

in the circumstances | Stock Exchange | general inquiry

Intersection

Stroke **N,** circle **S** may be intersected to represent the word **insurance:**

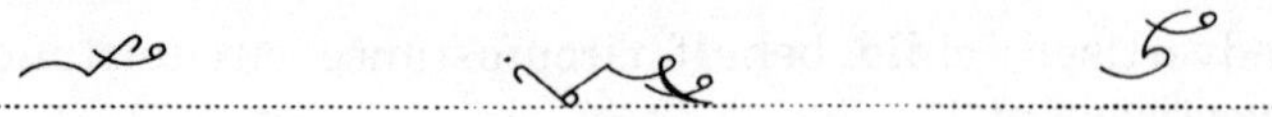

marine insurance | comprehensive insurance | national insurance

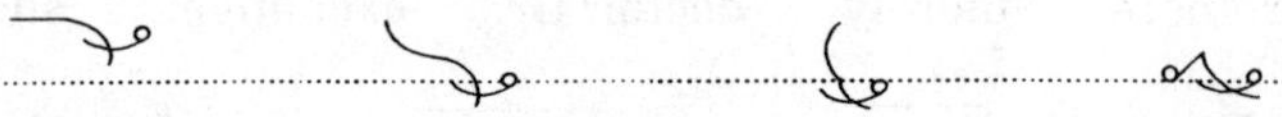

car insurance | fire insurance | theft insurance | certificate of insurance

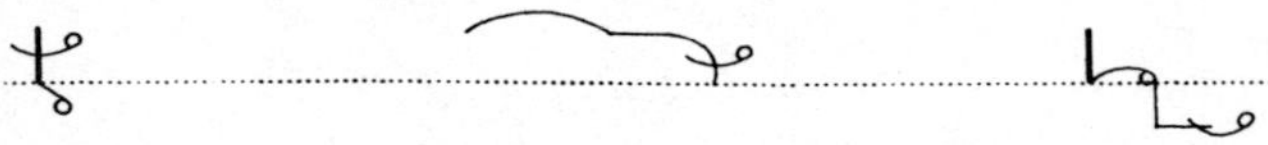

insurance depends | motor-car insurance | domestic insurance

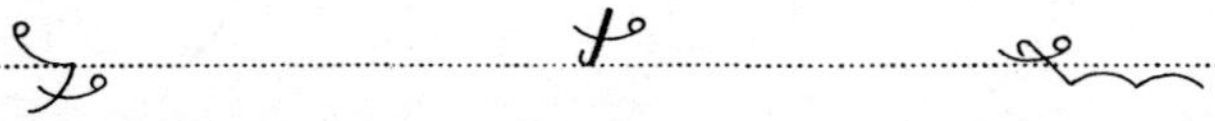

sufficient insurance | general insurance | insurance premium

Passage 7

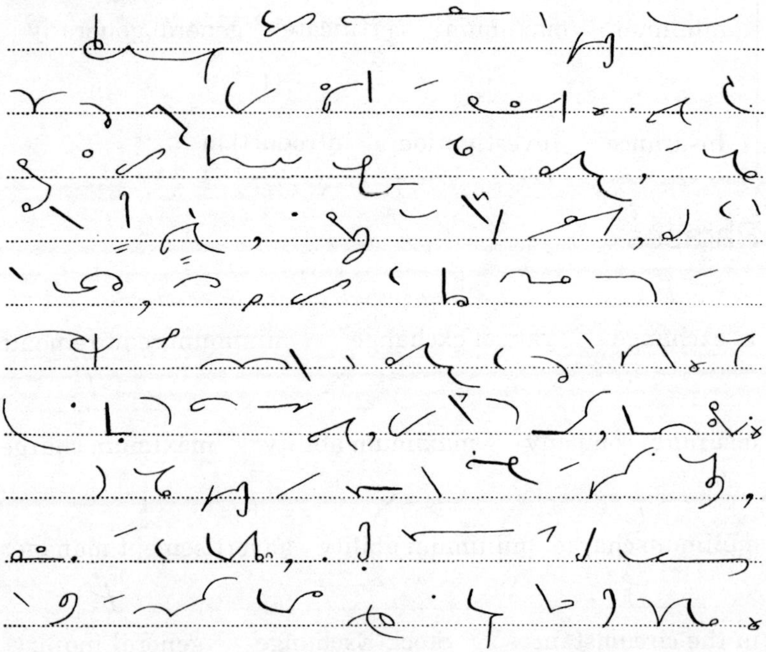

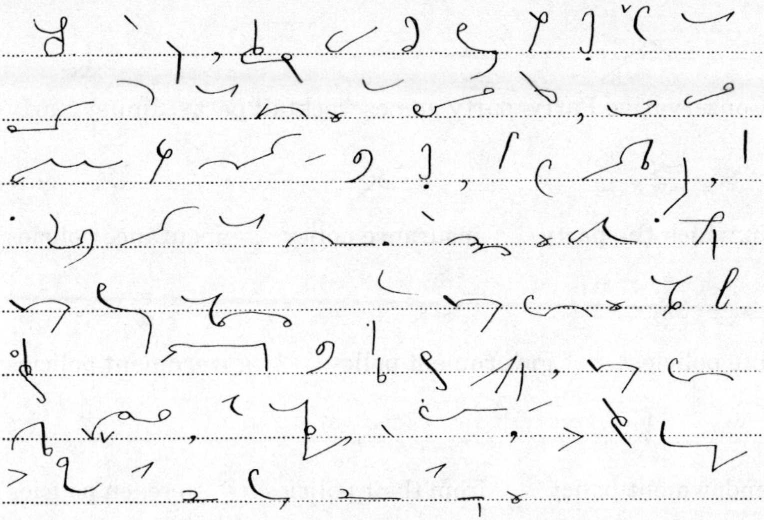

Suffix

The suffix **-ward** is expressed by half-length **W:**

forward forwarding forwarded henceforward

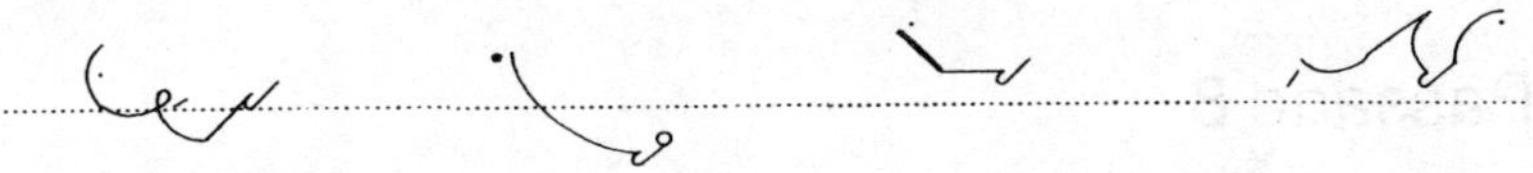

thenceforward afterwards backward northwardly

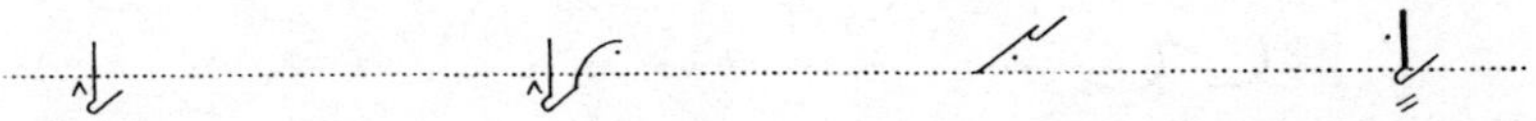

outward outwardly reward Edward

wayward straightforward straightforwardness

Intersections

P may be intersected to represent the words **party** and **policy:**

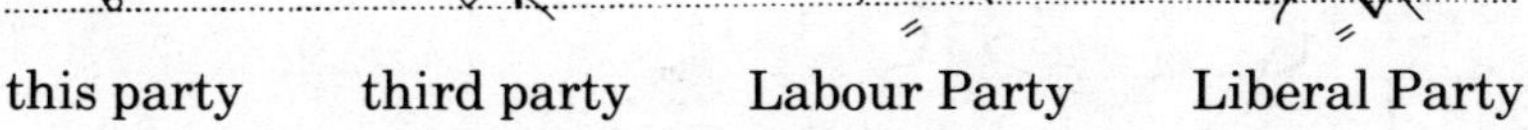

this party third party Labour Party Liberal Party

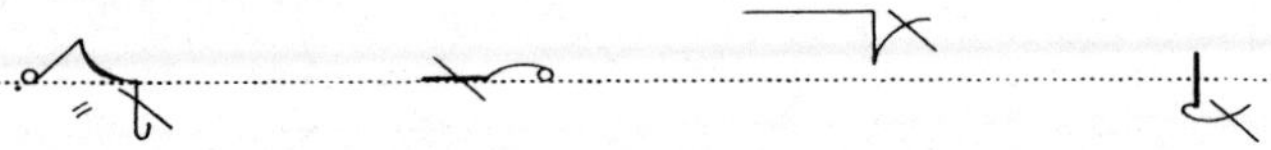

Conservative Party party games cocktail party dinner party

in which the party insurance policy insurance policies

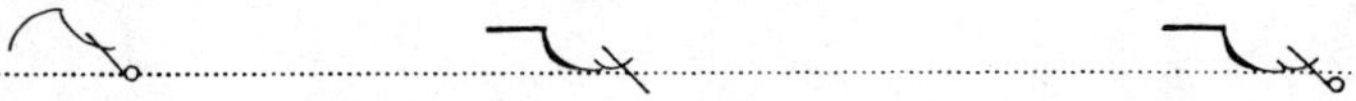

life policies government policy government policies

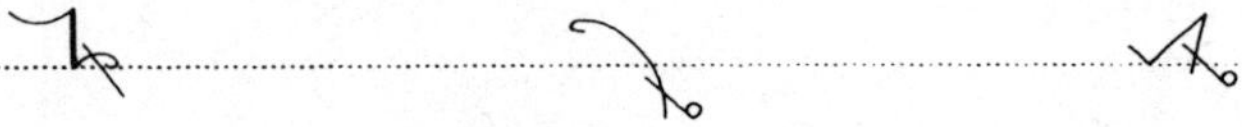

endowment policy from their policies to reach policies

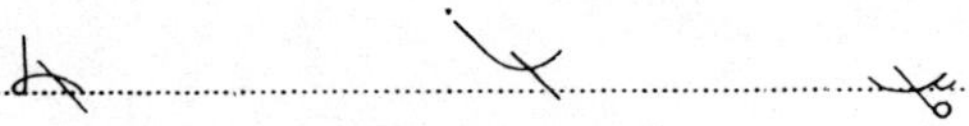

it is my policy company policy new policies

Note: The outline for the word **agent** is written ...... to distinguish it from **gentlemen** ....

Passage 8

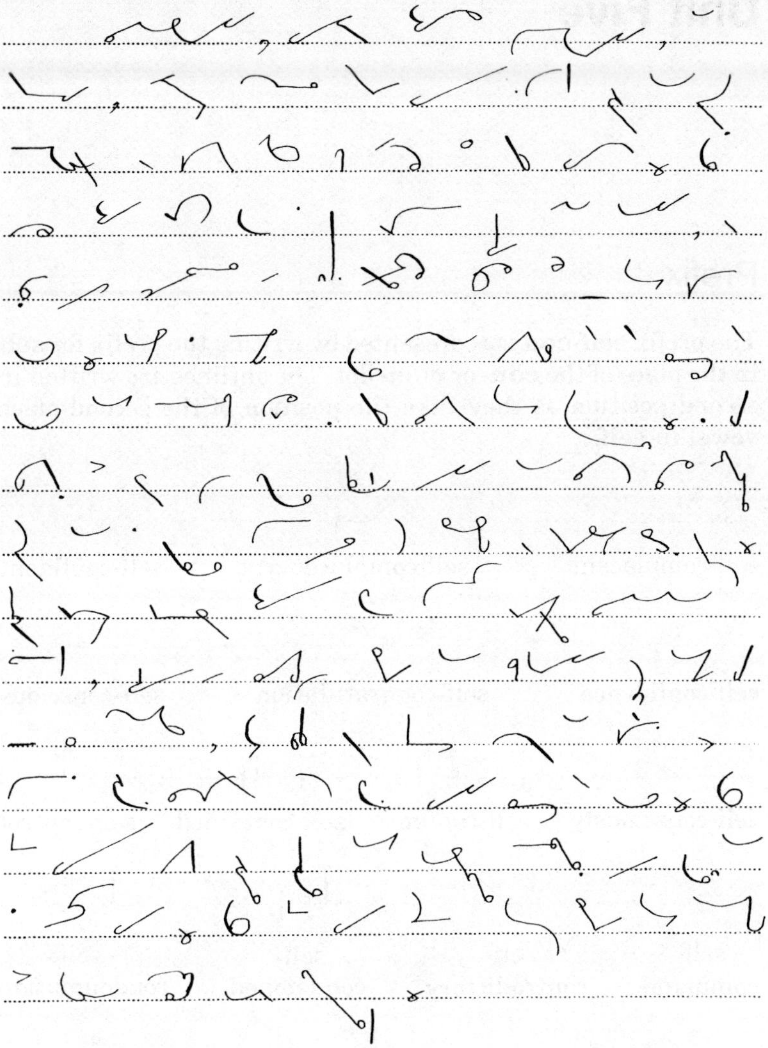

Unit Five

Prefix

The prefix **self-con** is represented by writing the prefix for **self** in the place of the **con-** or **com-** dot. The outlines are written in second position as they take the position of the second-place vowel in **self**:

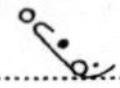
self-complacent

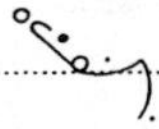
self-complacency

self-confident

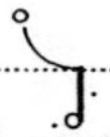
self-confidence

self-congratulation

self-conscious

self-consciously

self-content

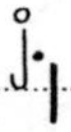
self-contained

self-control

self-command

self-contradictory

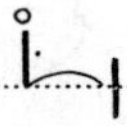
self-condemned

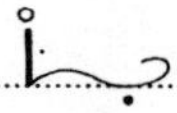
self-condemnation

self-consequence

self-conceited

self-considering

self-contempt

self-consumed

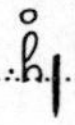
self-constituted

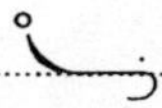
self-conviction

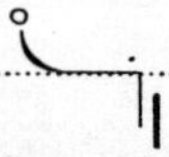
self-convicted

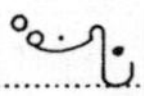
self-concentration

Short Forms and Derivatives

build/building generalization great liberty near

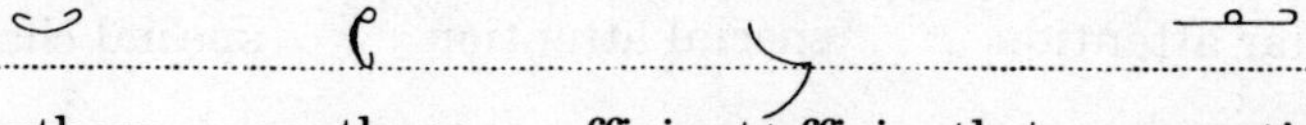

northern southern efficient/efficiently/efficiency executive

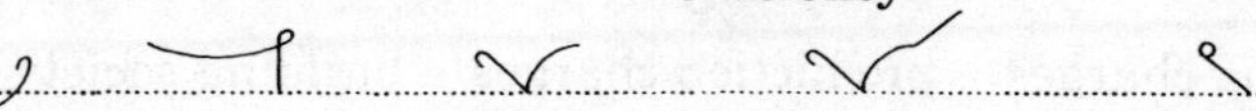

sure interest parliament parliamentary special/specially

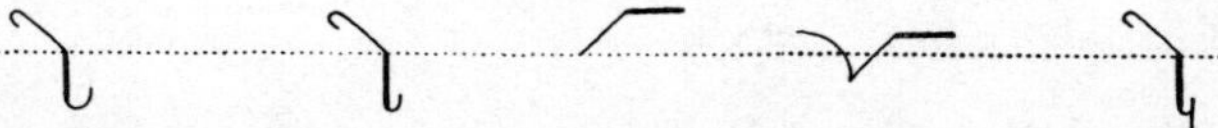

production productive regular irregular productivity

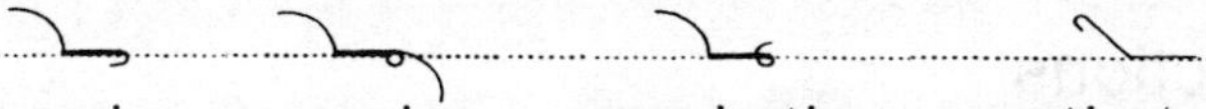

organize organizer organization practice/practise

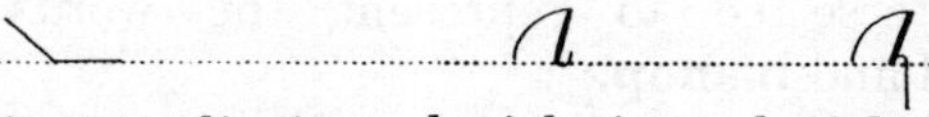

peculiar/peculiarity legislative legislature

Phrases

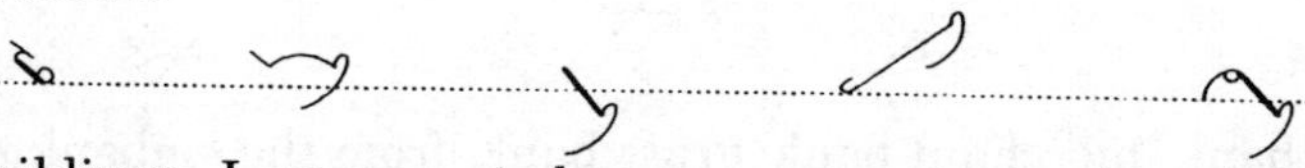

of buildings I am sure to be sure we are sure let us be sure

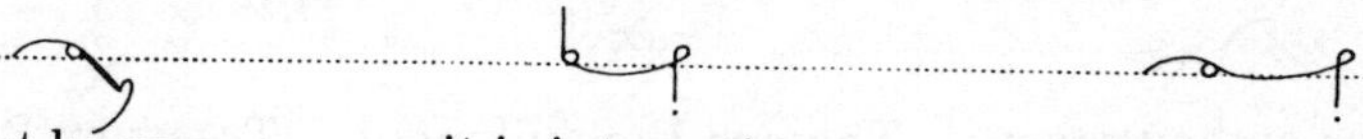

must be sure it is interesting most interesting

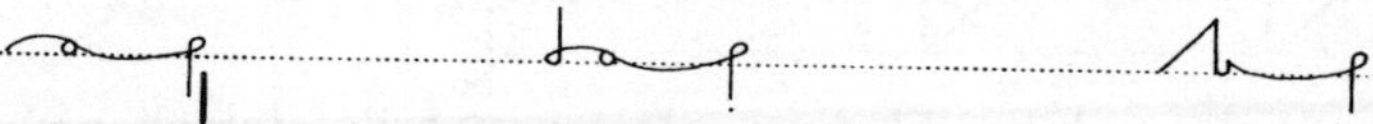

most interested it is most interesting rate of interest

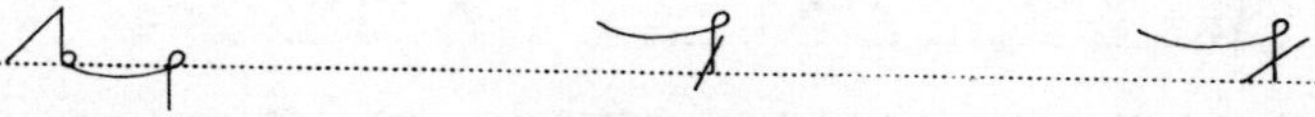

rates of interest interest charge interest required

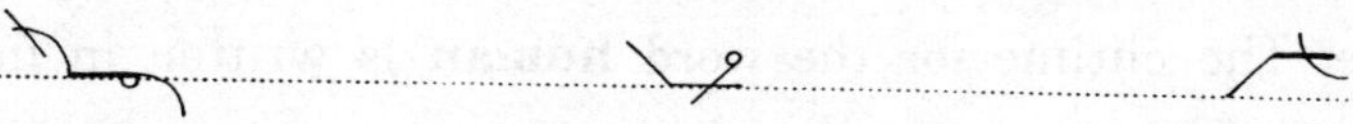

party organizer peculiar requirements regular form

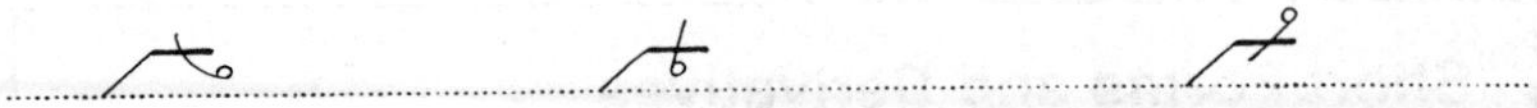

regular forms   regular charges   regular requirements

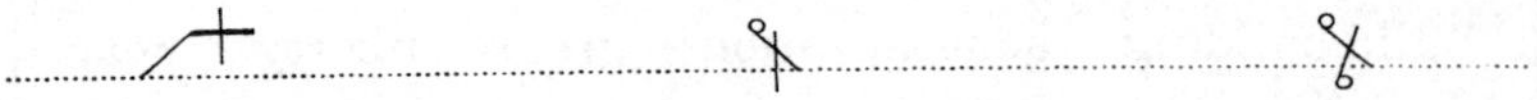

regular attention   special attention   special charges

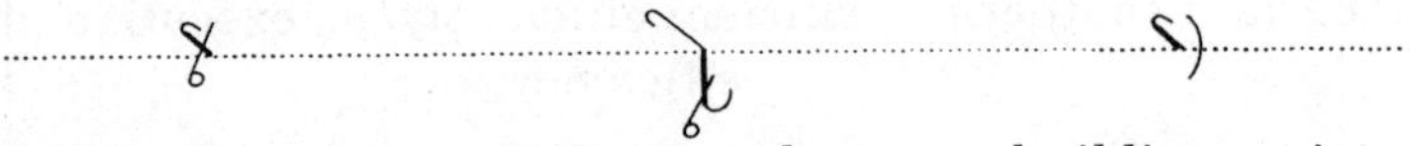

building charges   production charges   building society

Two useful phrases are:

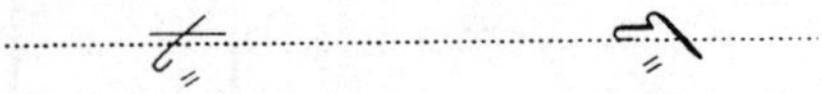

United Kingdom   Great Britain

Intersections

B may be intersected to represent the words **bank, -bankment, bill** and **bishop:**

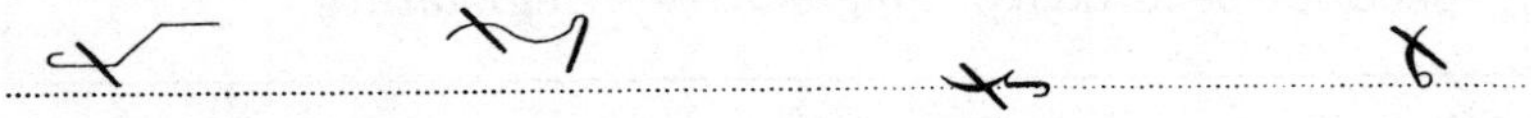

bank clerk   bank manager   Bank of England   this bank

your bank   merchant bank   grass bank   from the embankment

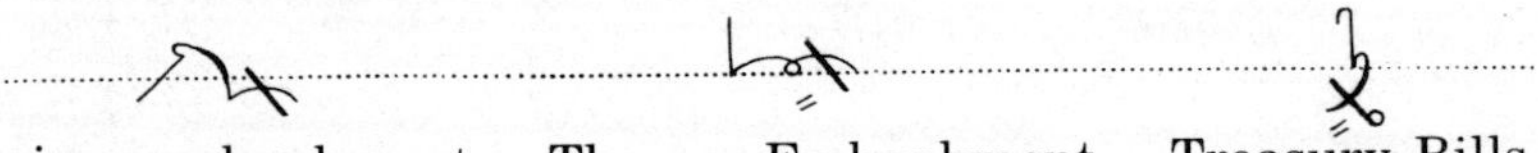

river embankment   Thames Embankment   Treasury Bills

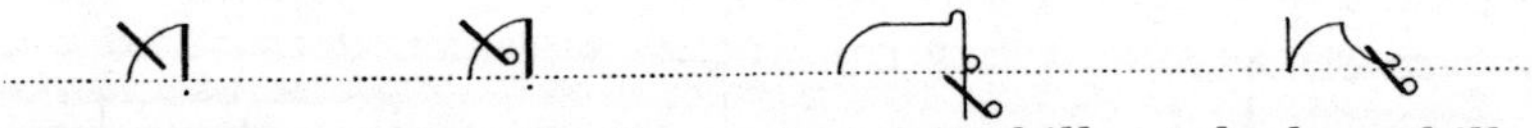

bill of lading   bills of lading   electricity bills   telephone bills

any other bills   local bishop   Bishop of London

Note: The outline for the word **human** is written in first position  to distinguish it from **humane** .

Passage 9

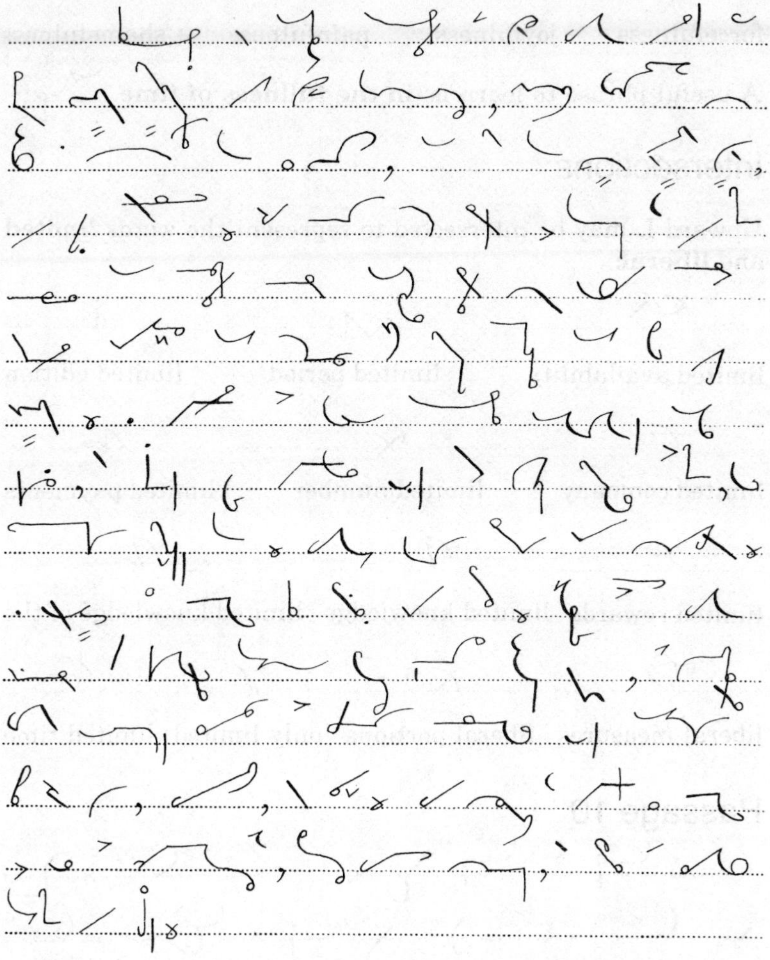

Suffix

The suffix **-fulness** is represented by a disjoined stroke **F** and circle **S**:

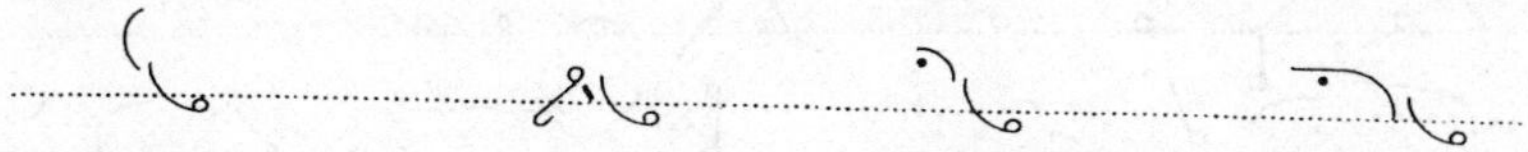

thankfulness usefulness artfulness carefulness

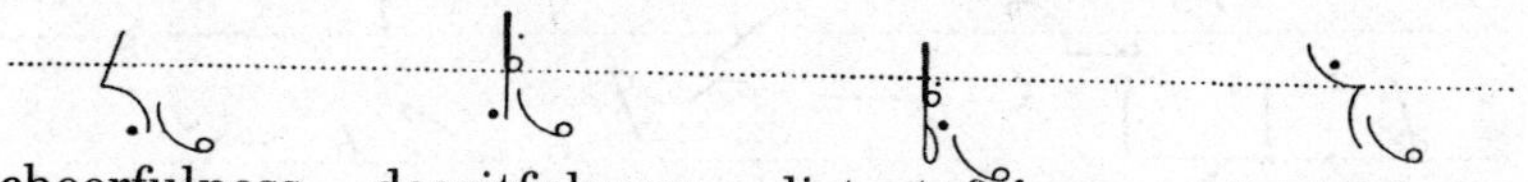

cheerfulness deceitfulness distastefulness faithfulness

forcefulness joyfulness painfulness shamefulness

A useful phrase to learn is: **in the fullness of time**

Intersections

Upward **L** may be intersected to represent the words **limited** and **liberal:**

limited availability limited period limited edition

limited company limited number limited payments

limited rewards limited knowledge limited knowledge of the

liberal measures liberal portions only limited limited time

Passage 10

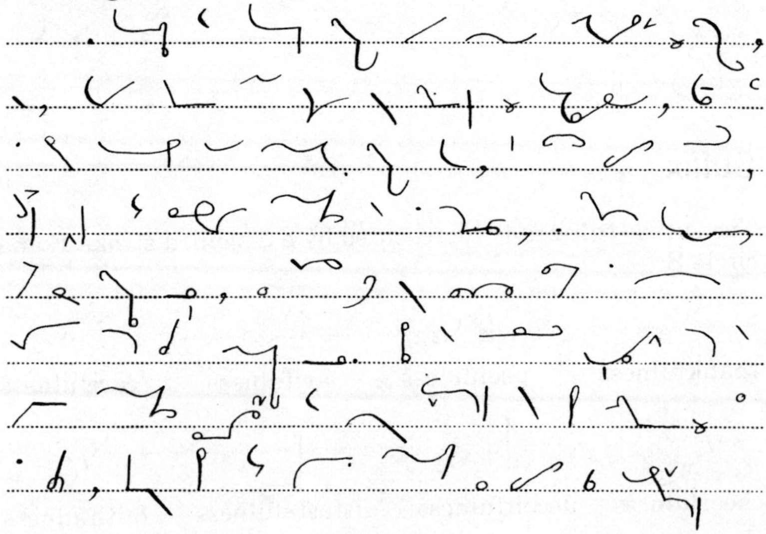

Unit Six

Suffix

The suffix **-yard** is expressed by half-length **Y:**

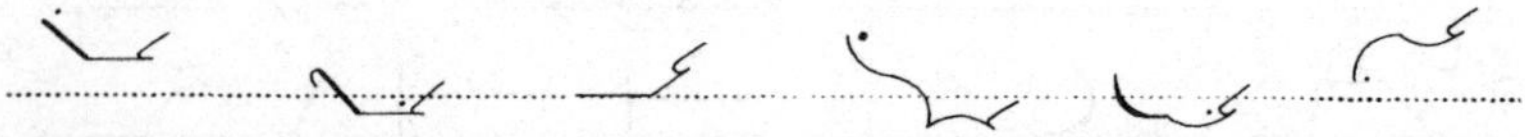

backyard brickyard courtyard farmyard vineyard lanyard

Note: The outline for the word **notable** is written to distinguish it from **noble**.

Short Forms and Derivatives

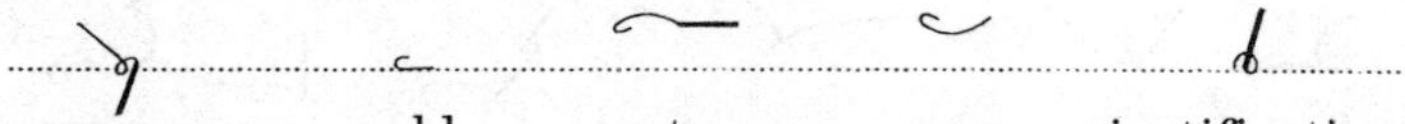

passenger cold mortgage nor justification

opportunity perform performance tell under

understand understood young younger youngster

principal/principally/ principle unprincipled speak valuation

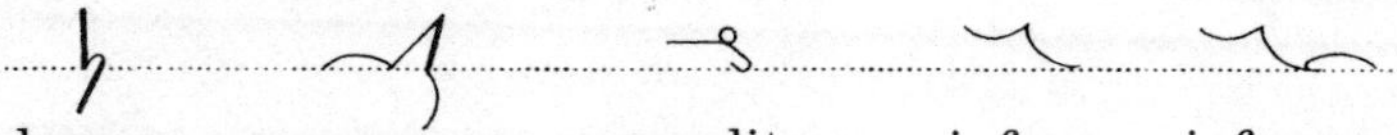

danger emergency expenditure inform informer

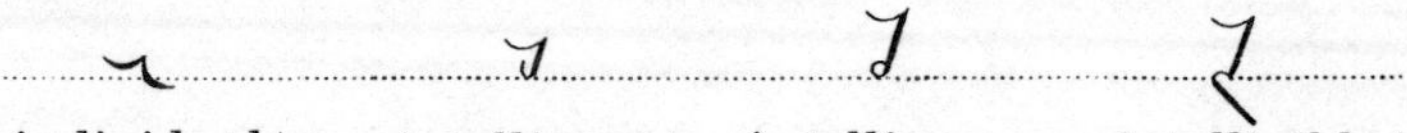

individual/ individually intelligent/ intelligently intelligence intelligible/ intelligibly

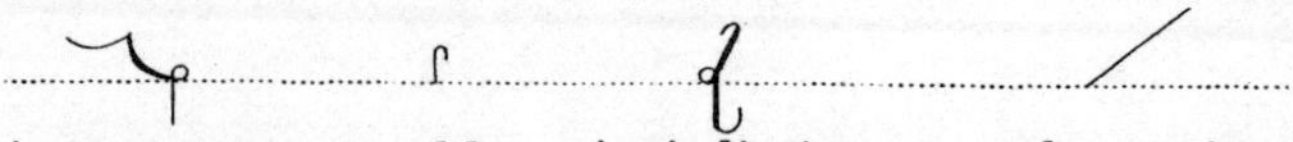

investment told jurisdiction rather/writer

Note: The outline for the word **dangerous** is written … to distinguish it from **dangers** …, and the outline for the word **prowess** is written … to distinguish it from **principles** … .

Phrases

passenger requirements   passengers require   principal charges

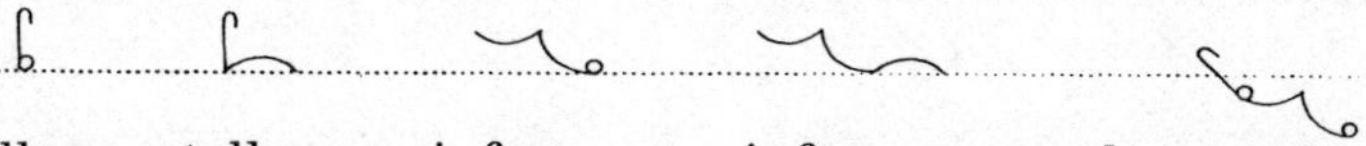

tell us   tell me   inform us   inform me   please inform us

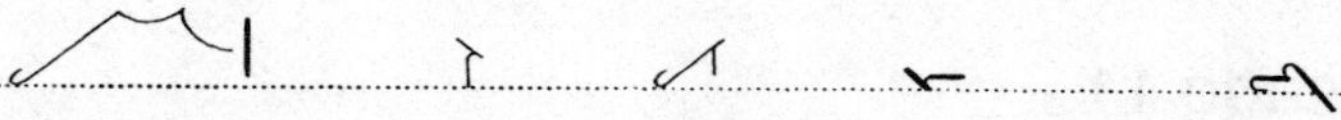

we are informed   I told   we told   too great   great number

great number of the   great part   great part (of) the

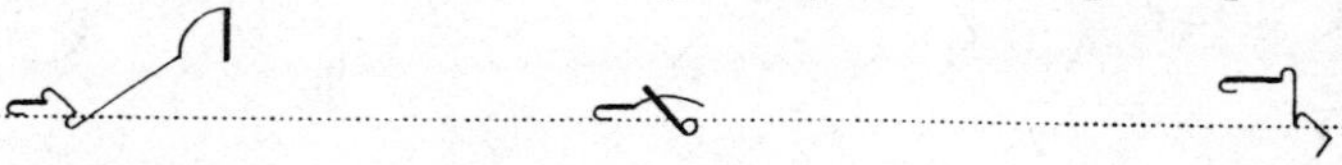

great part of the world   great embankments   greater part of the

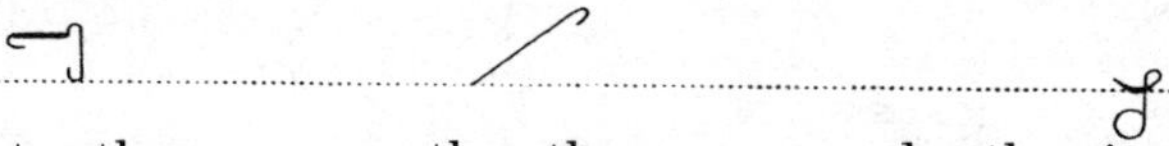

greater than   rather than   under the circumstances

expenditure required   cold morning   young men

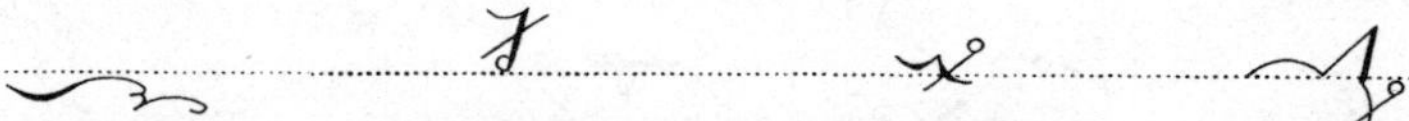

young men and women   intelligence required   individual requirements   emergency requirements

Phrasing Principles

The half-length **Y** for the suffix **yard** may also be used in phrasing:

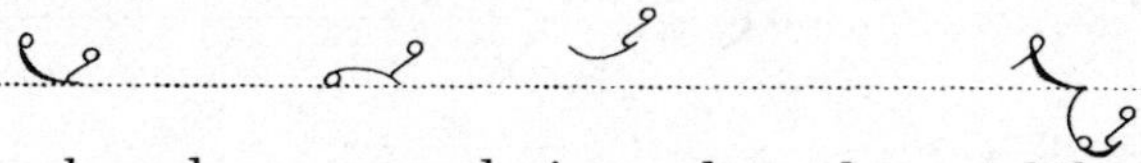

several yards   some yards   in yards   and several thousand yards

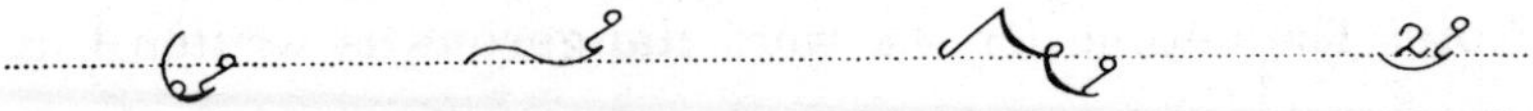

thousand yards   many yards   we have several yards   200 yards

The outline for **nor** may be omitted in some useful phrases:

neither more nor less 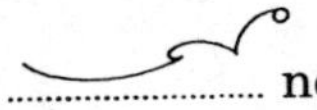 neither this nor that 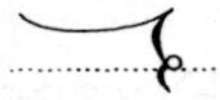

A time-saving phrase is: at any rate 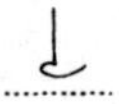

Passage 11

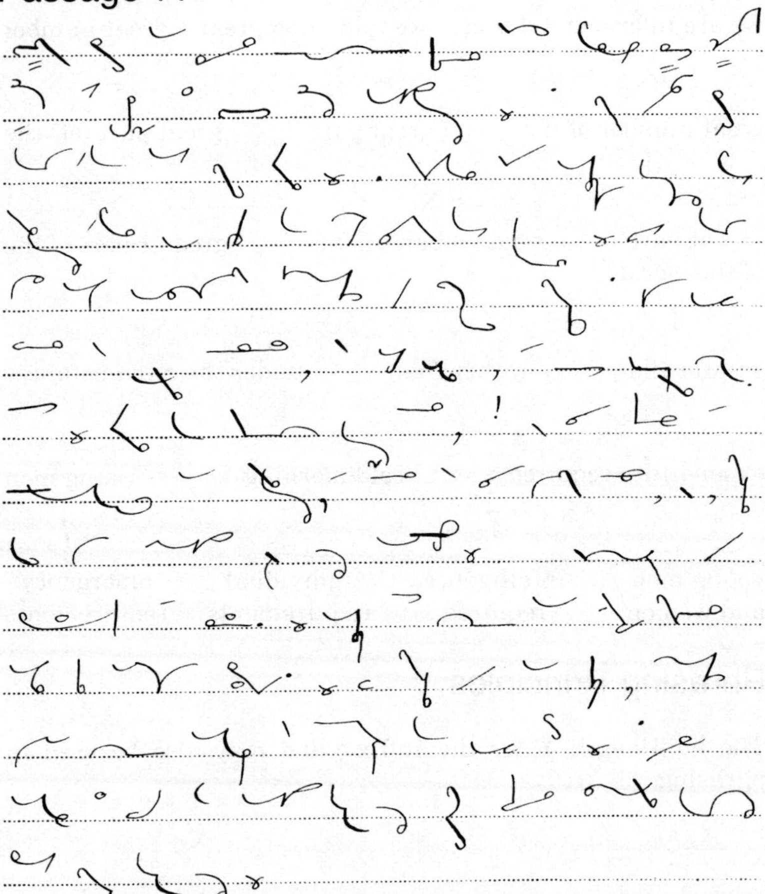

Intersections

K may be intersected or written close to another stroke to represent the words **council, capital** and **captain,** as well as **company**. Circle **S** may also be added to the intersected **K:**

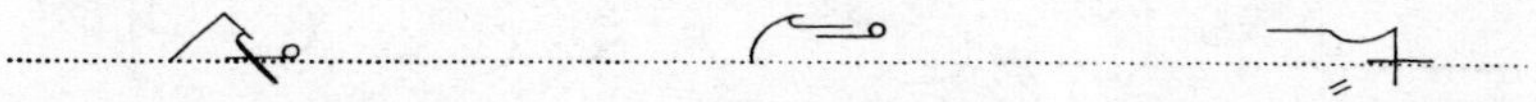

reputable companies | local councils | County Council

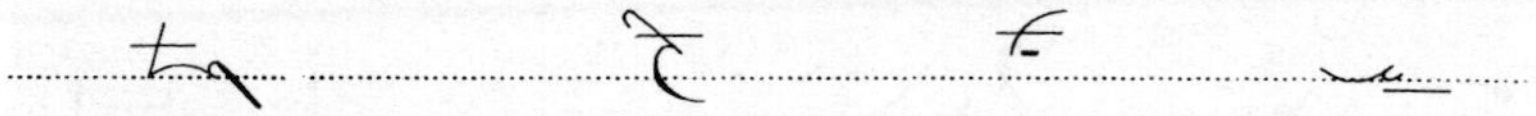

council chamber | council approval | law council | new capital

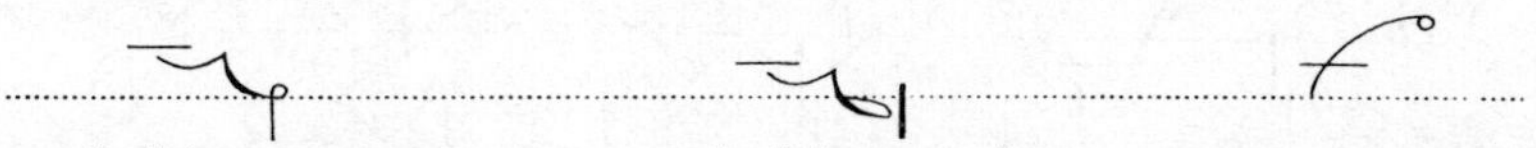

capital investment | capital invested | capital letters

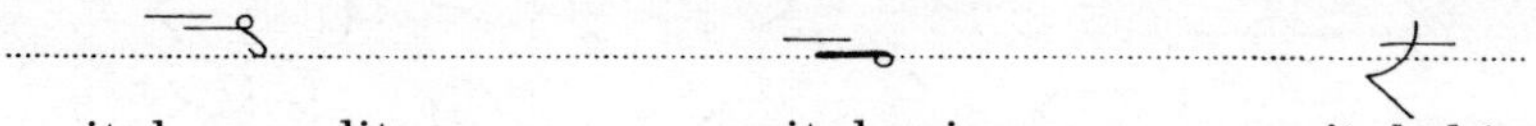

capital expenditure | capital gains | capital ship

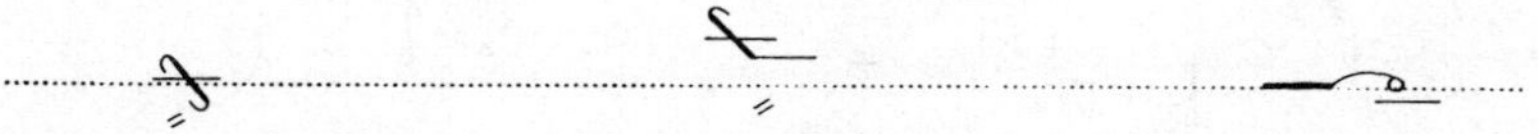

Captain Brown | Captain Black | games captain

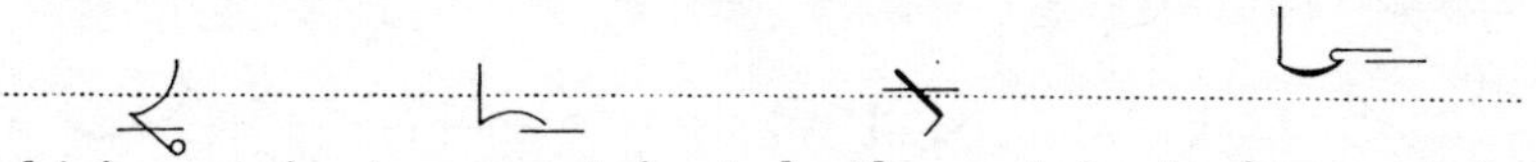

ship's captain | team captain | to be the captain | tanker captain

Note: The outline for the word **inevitable** is written 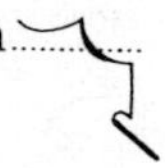 to distinguish it from **unavoidable** 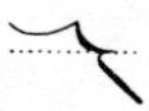.

Passage 12

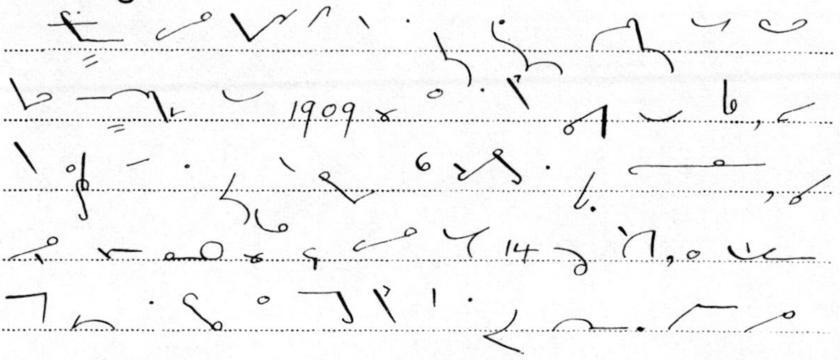

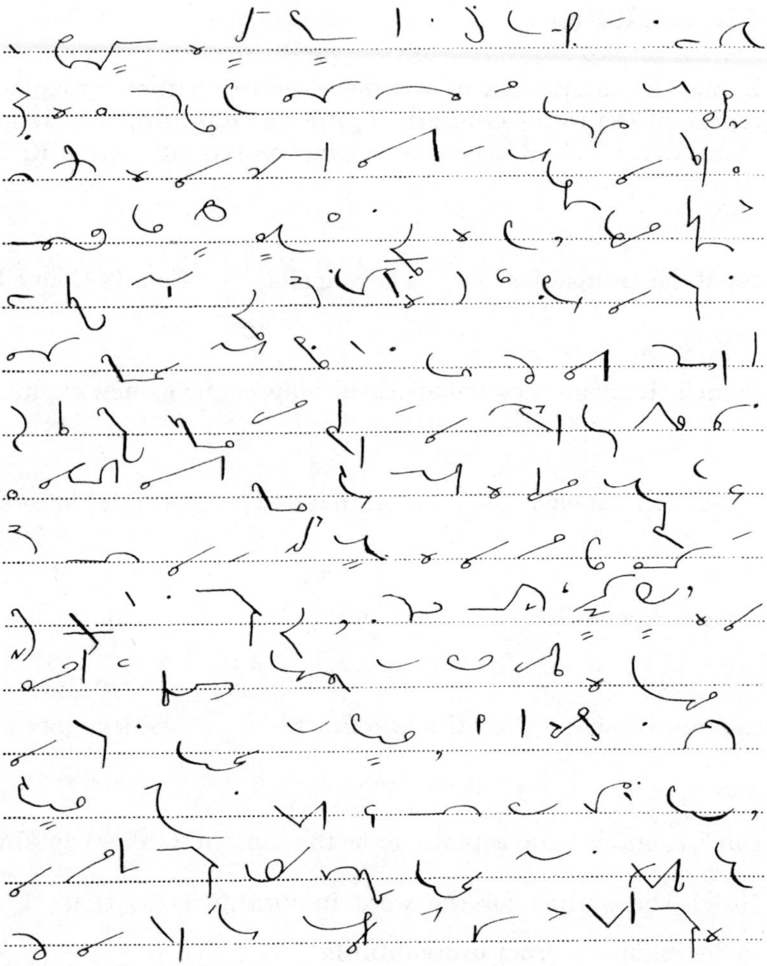

Unit Seven

Suffixes

The suffixes **-lessness** and **-lousness** are represented by writing a disjoined upward **L** and circle **S:**

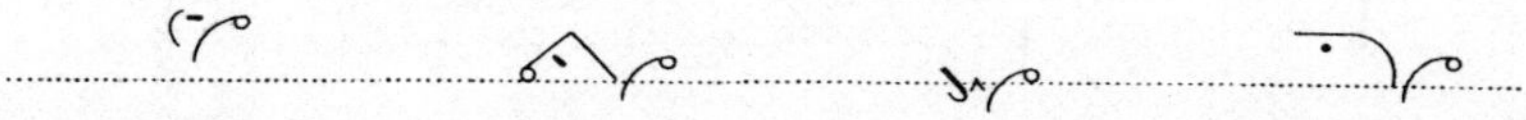

thoughtlessness	hopelessness	boundlessness	carelessness

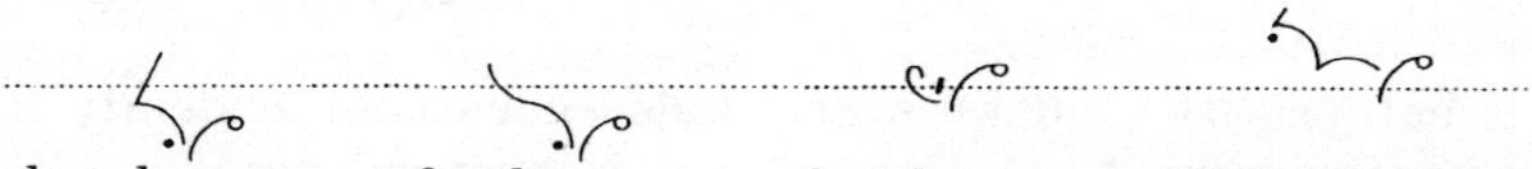

cheerlessness	fearlessness	fruitlessness	harmlessness

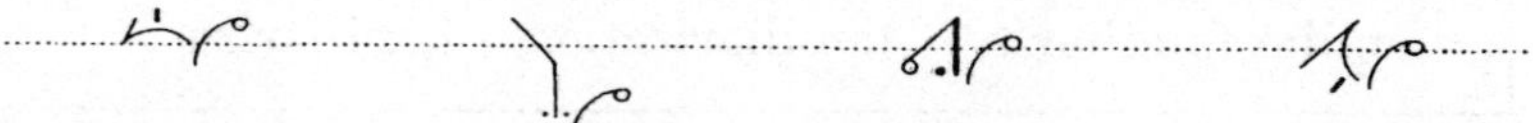

homelessness	pitilessness	heedlessness	ruthlessness

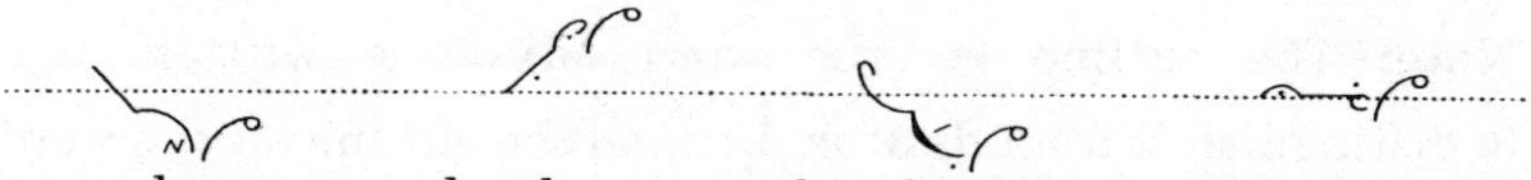

powerlessness	relentlessness	frivolousness	meticulousness

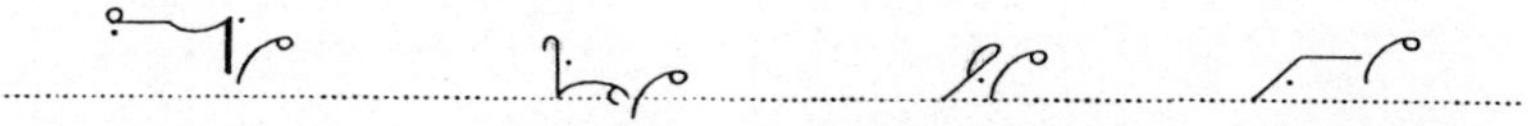

scandalousness	tremulousness	restlessness	recklessness

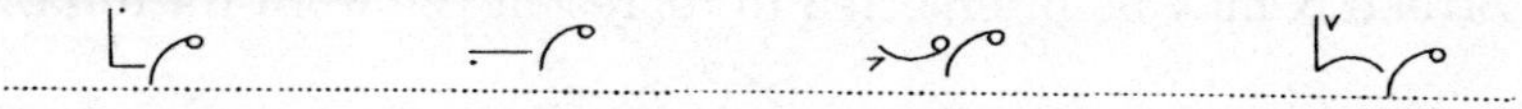

tactlessness	callousness	noiselessness	timelessness

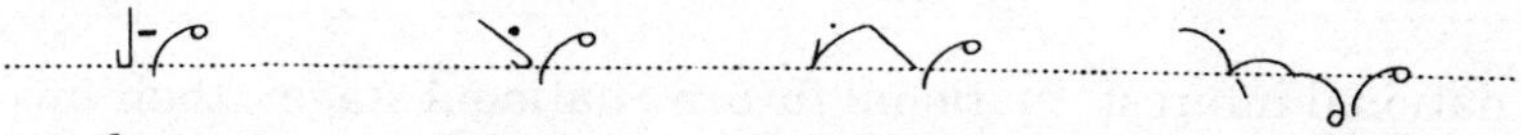

tonelessness	painlessness	helplessness	remorselessness

Short Forms and Derivatives

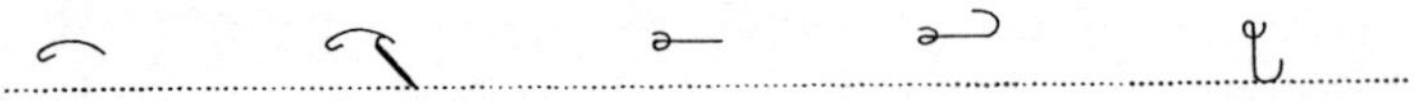

remark | remarkable/ remarkably | inscribe | inscription | instruction

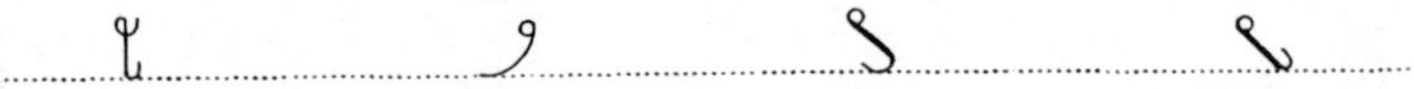

instructive | selfish/ selfishness | subjection | subjective

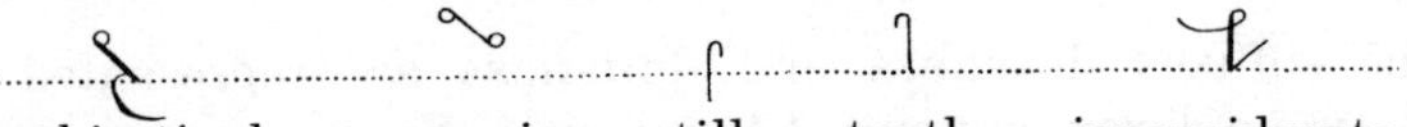

subjectively | surprise | till | truth | inconsiderate

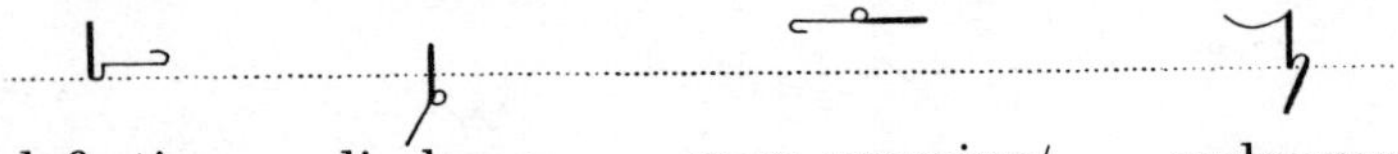

defective | discharge | cross-examine/ cross-examination | endanger

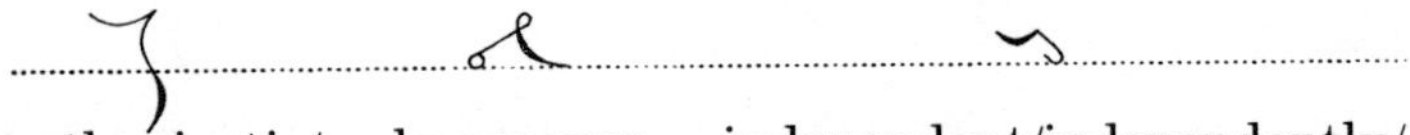

enthusiastic/ enthusiasm | howsoever | independent/independently/ independence

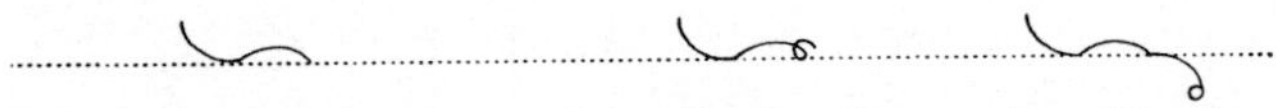

familiar/familiarity | familiarization | familiarize

Note: The outline for the word **editor** is written 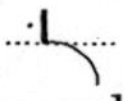 to distinguish it from **debtor** 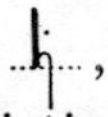, and the outline for the word **queer** is written  to distinguish it from **clear** 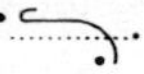.

Intersection

Stroke **N** may be intersected to represent the word **national:**

national economy | National Health | national survey

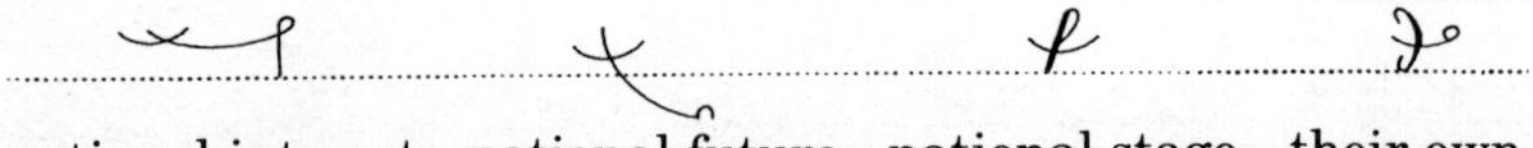

national interest | national future | national stage | their own nationals

foreign national   national expenditure   national average

Passage 13

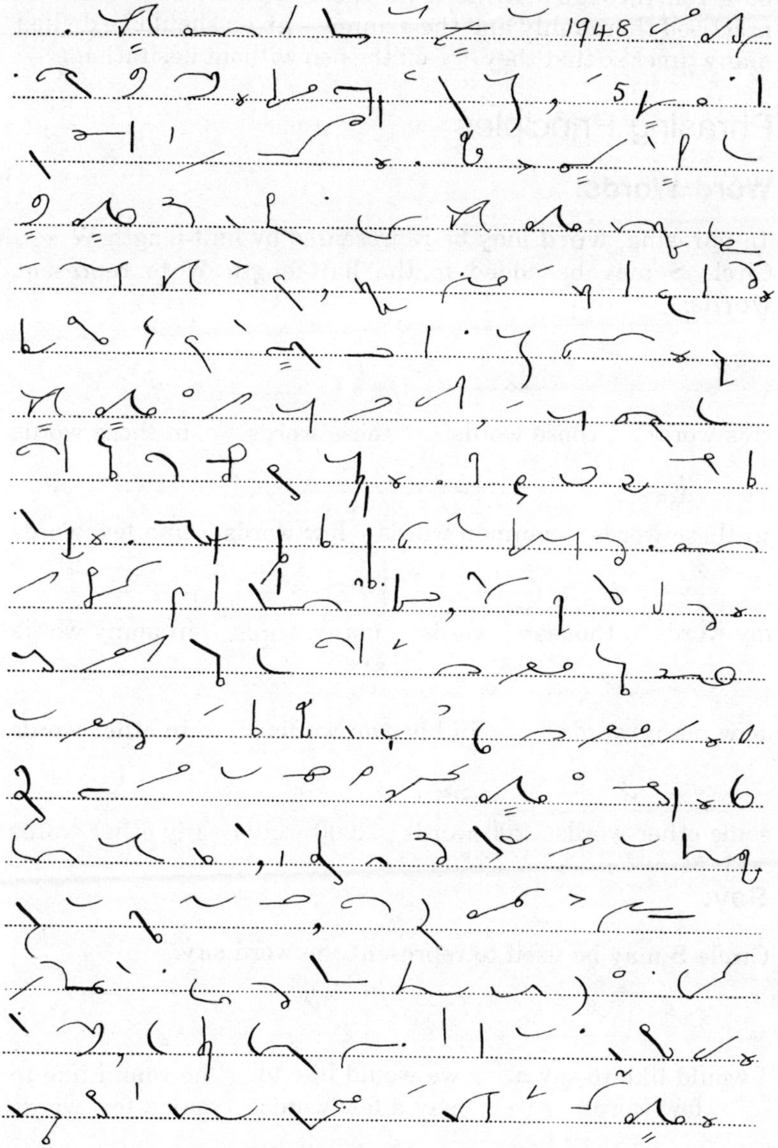

Phrases

The use of advanced phrasing can be most beneficial to the potential high-speed writer provided the principles of phrasing are thoroughly understood and adhered to. It is the skilled application of the principles that marks the trained writer. The main principles of phrasing applied to Pitman 2000 Shorthand appear in *Phrase Book* but further principles will continue to be given throughout this text. These should be learned and practised thoroughly and the examples given should be drilled many times so that they 'fly' off the pen without hesitation.

Phrasing Principles

Word/Words:

In phrasing, **word** may be represented by half-length **W**  . Circle **S** may be added to the half-length **W** to represent **words:**

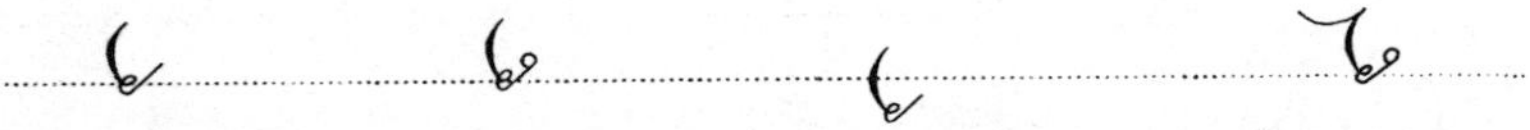

this word | those words | these words | in those words

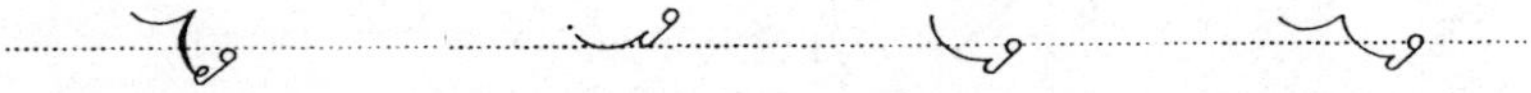

in these words | common words | few words | in a few words

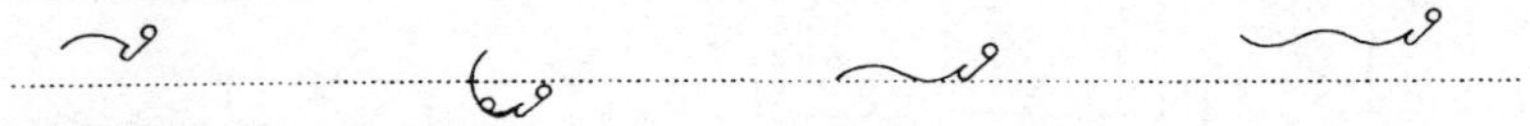

my words | thousand words | many words | in many words

how many words | in his own words | in other words

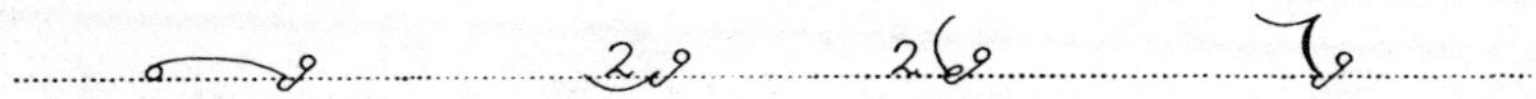

some other words | 200 words | 2,000 words | any other words

Say:

Circle **S** may be used to represent the word **say**:

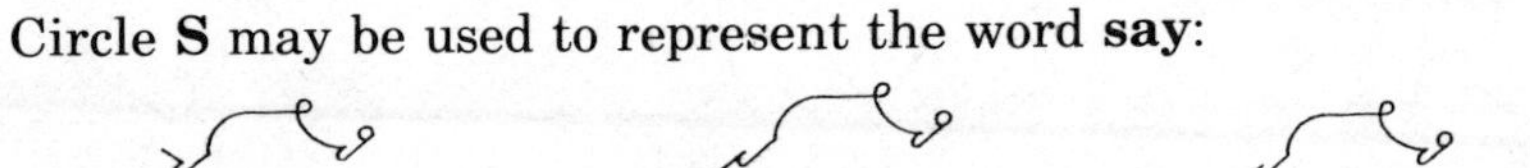

I would like to say a few words | we would like to say a few words | he would like to say a few words

to say a few words — I have to say that — we have to say that

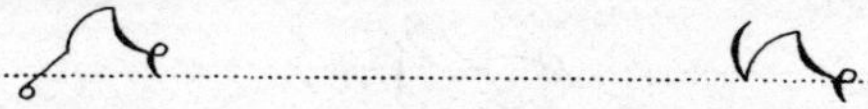

he will have to say that — they will have to say that

Per:

P, hook **R** may be used to represent **per** in phrases:

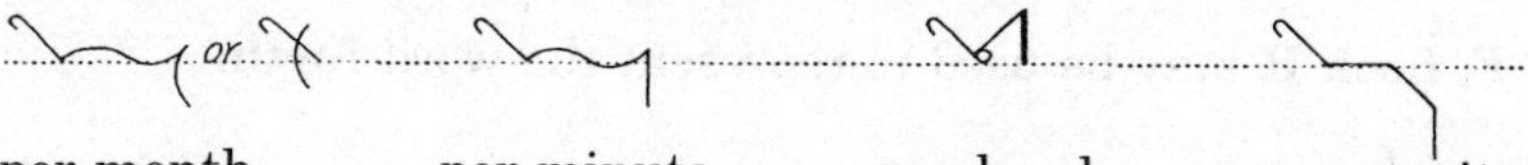

per month — per minute — per head — per capita

Park:

P, hook **R** may be used to represent the word **park:**

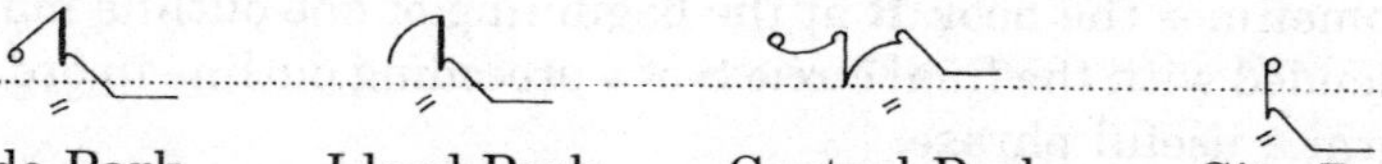

Hyde Park — Lloyd Park — Central Park — City Park

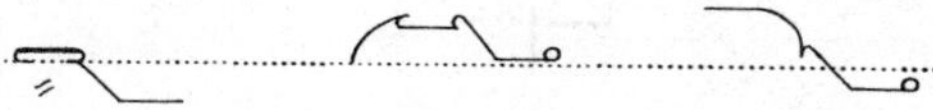

Green Park — local parks — car parks

As – Hook R:

The circle **S** blends with hook **R** to straight strokes to form many useful phrases:

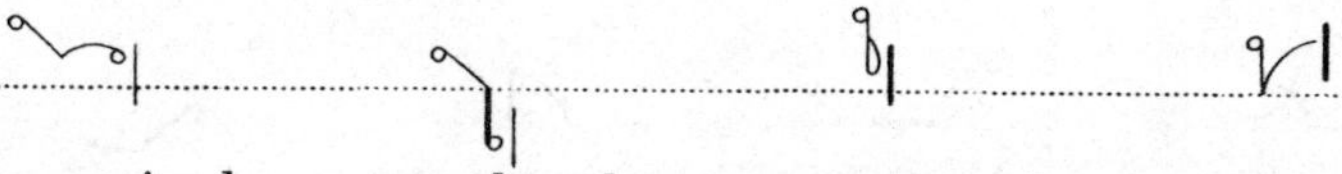

as promised — as produced — as contrasted — as controlled

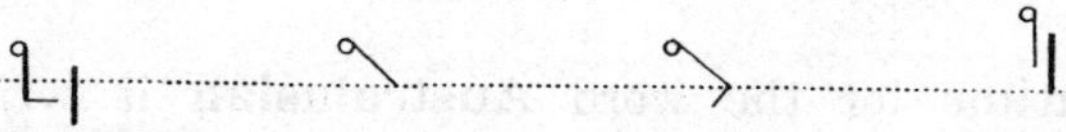

as directed — as per — as per the — as tried

Assure:

SH, hook **R** may be used to represent the word **assure:**

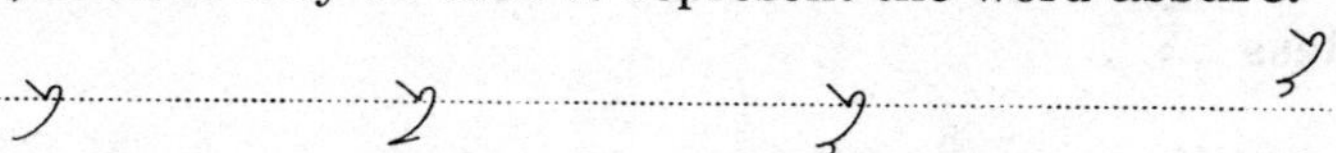

to assure — to assure the — to assure you — I assure you

we assure you | they assure us | we are assured

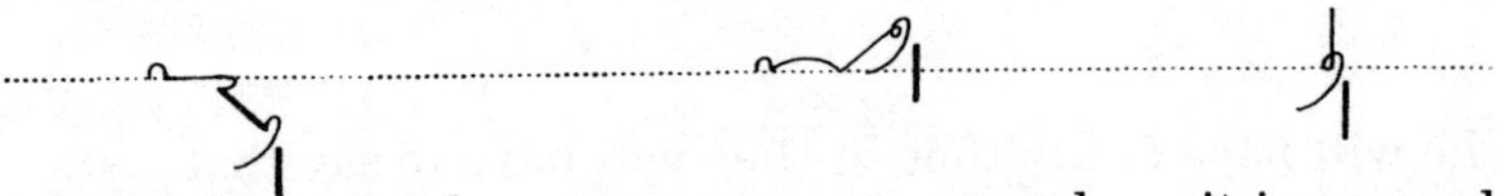

you can be assured | you may rest assured | it is assured

Forth:

F, hook **R** may be used to represent the word **forth:**

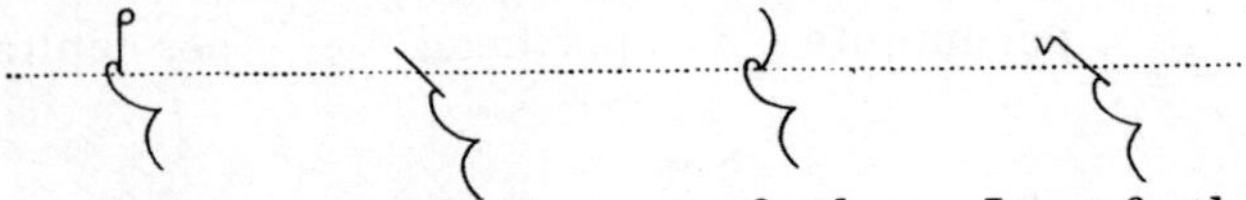

set forth | put forth | so forth | I put forth

Sometimes the hook **R** at the beginning of one outline may be blended with the final circle **S** of a preceding outline in order to form a useful phrase:

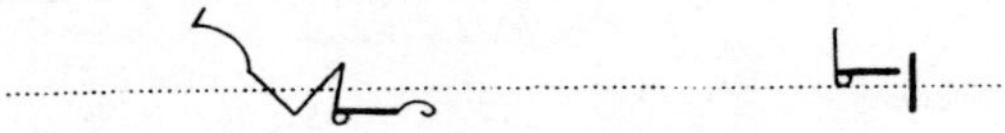

hire purchase agreement | it is agreed

Intersection

Stroke **F** may be intersected to represent the word **forth:**

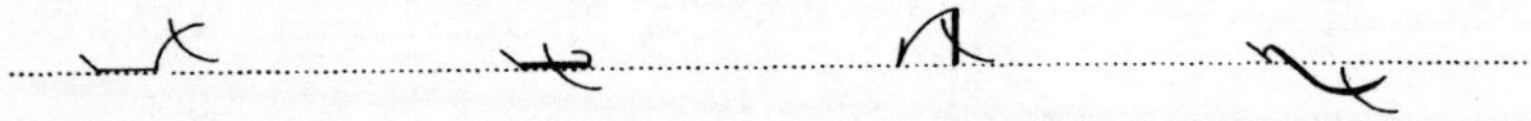

to call forth | to give forth | hold forth | to bring forth

Note: The outline for the word **Australasian** is written  to distinguish it from **Australian** 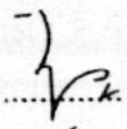, and the outline for the word **needless** is written to distinguish it from **endless** 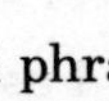.

A useful phrase is: **needless to say** .

Passage 14

Unit Eight

Short Forms and Derivatives

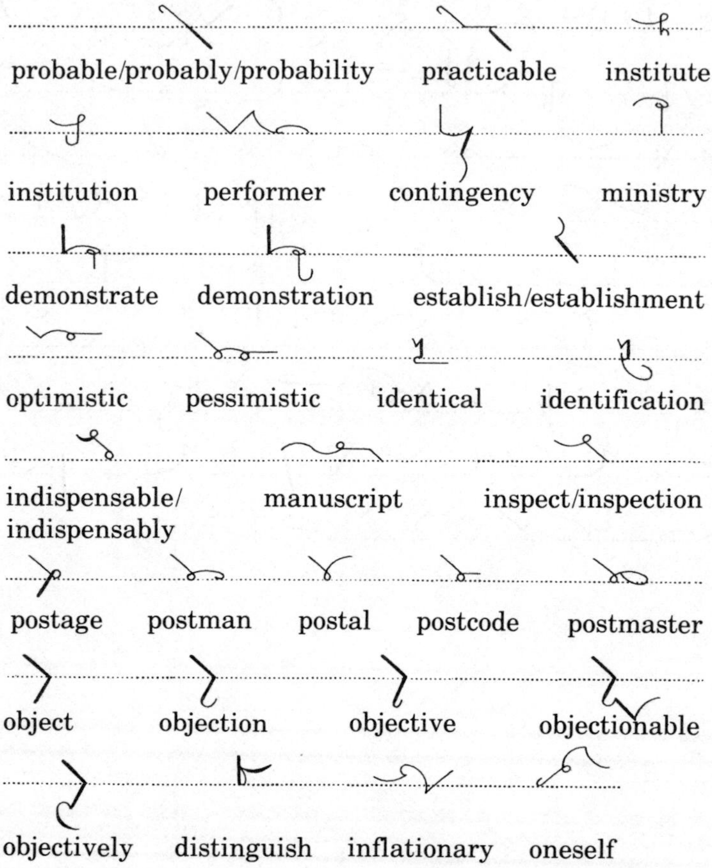

Note: The outline for the word **decease** is written ...... to distinguish it from **disease** ......, and the outline for the word **escapade** is written ...... to distinguish it from **escape** ....

Intersections

Circle **S** and **M** may be intersected to represent the word **similar:**

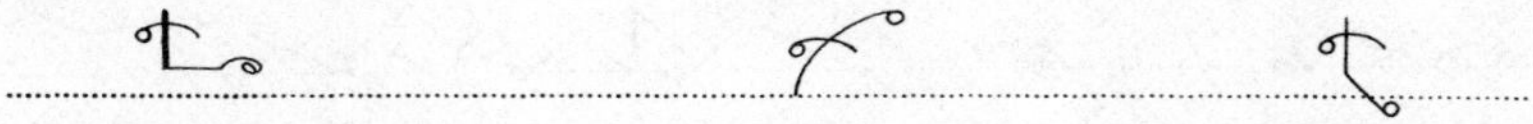

similar documents — similar letters — similar types

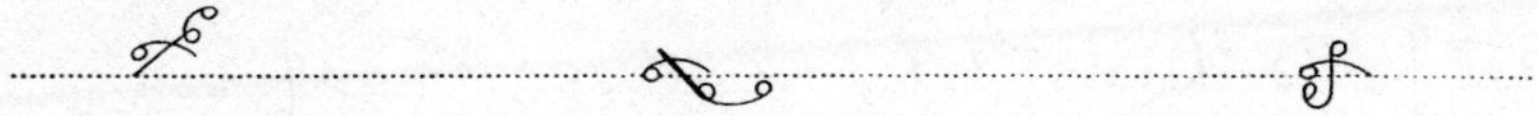

similar results — similar business — similar situations

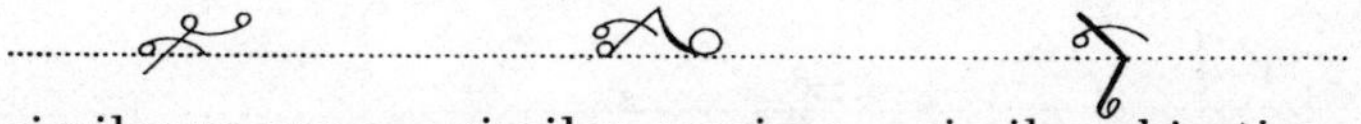

similar reasons — similar services — similar objectives

Circle **S** and upward **R** 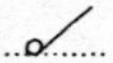 may be intersected to represent the word **conservative**:

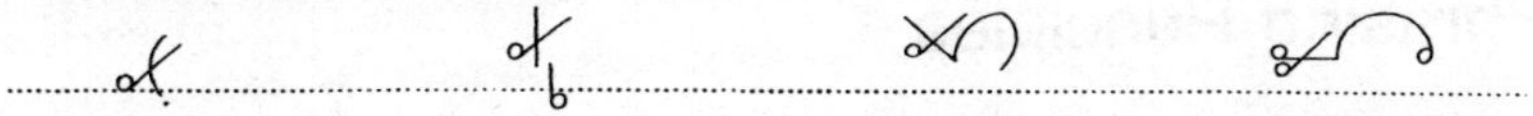

conservative thinking — conservative attitudes — conservative policy — conservative scholars

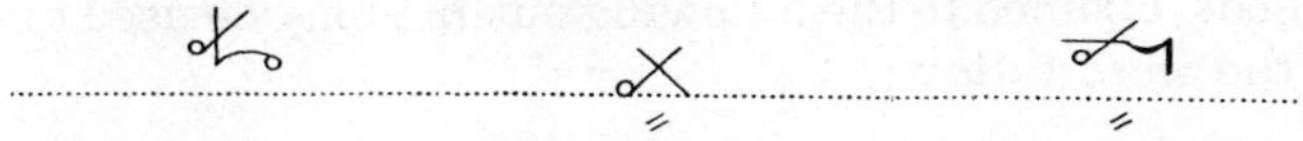

conservative times — Conservative Party — Conservative candidate

Passage 15

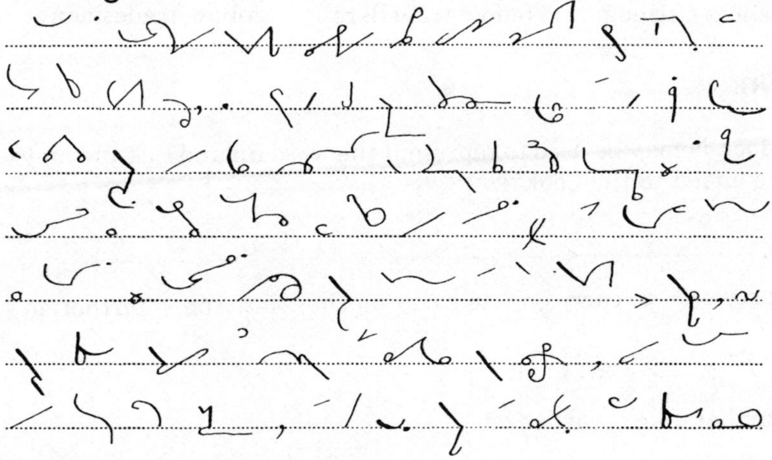

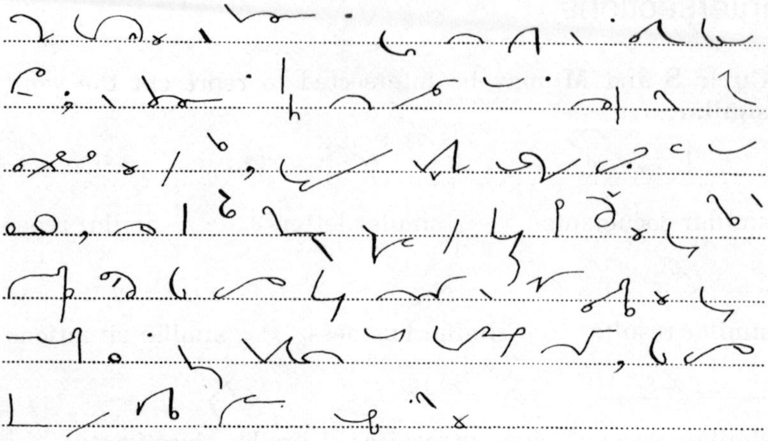

Phrasing Principles

Fellow:

Stroke **F,** hook **L** joined to the following outline may be used to represent the word **fellow:**

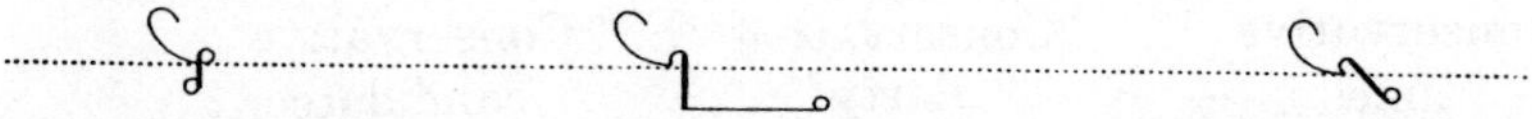

fellow students fellow directors fellow members

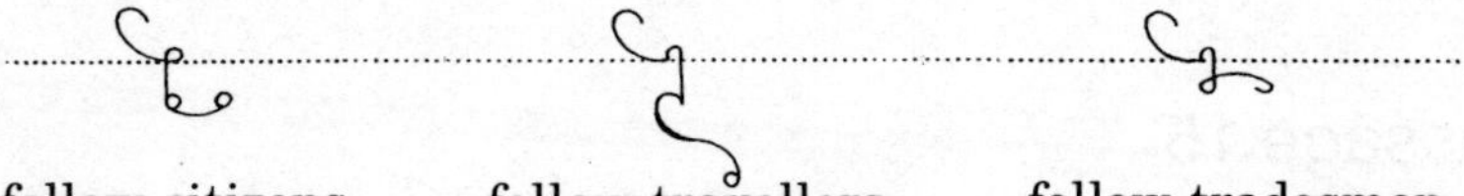

fellow citizens fellow travellers fellow tradesmen

On:

Hook **N** may be used to represent the word **on** and tick **the** may be added to the hook:

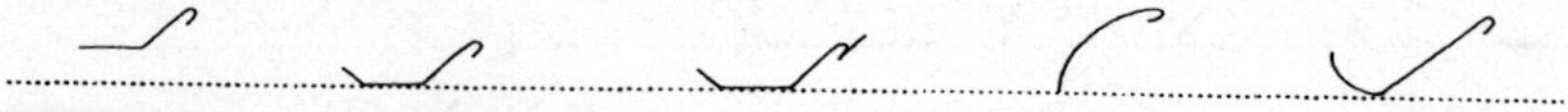

carry on to carry on to carry on the later on further on

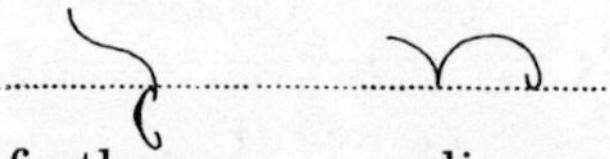

farther on earlier on

Information:

The use of the **shun hook** is made in the following phrases to represent the word **information**:

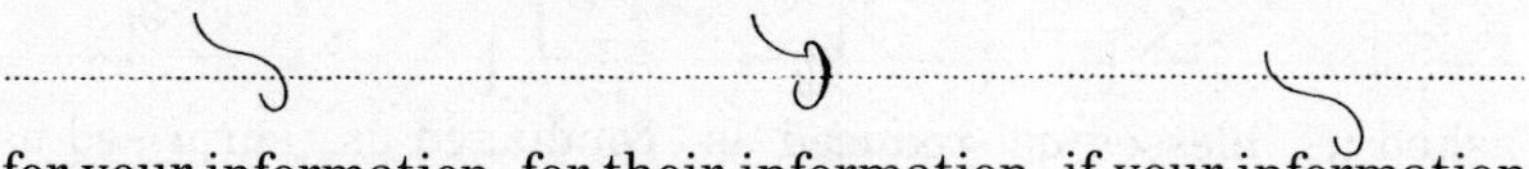

for your information for their information if your information

but the short form is retained in:

for his information any information further information

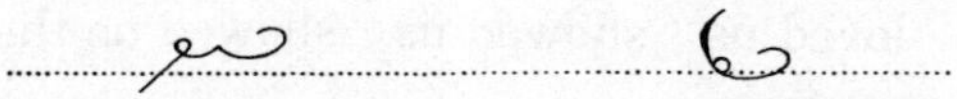

recent information this information

The direction of the **shun hook** in phrases may differ from the direction taken in an outline standing alone:

Occasion:

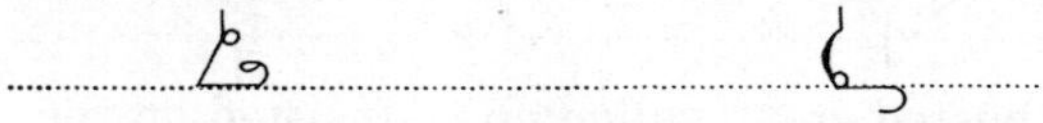

on such occasions **but** on this occasion

Section:

in this section in these sections on this section

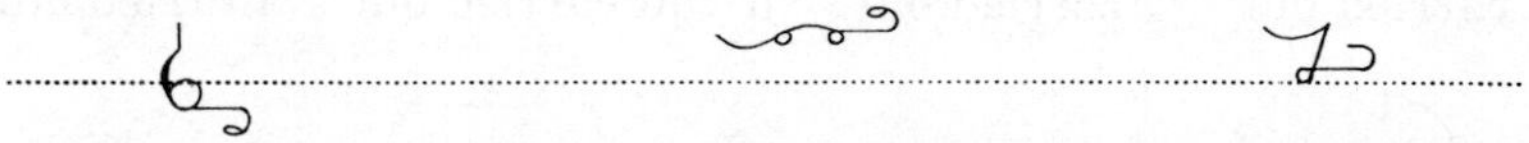

on these sections **but** in some sections in which section

Additions to disjoined T or D in past tenses

In past tenses of weak verbs, the circle **S** may be added to a disjoined **T** or **D** to represent **us** and tick **the** may be added to the circle **S**:

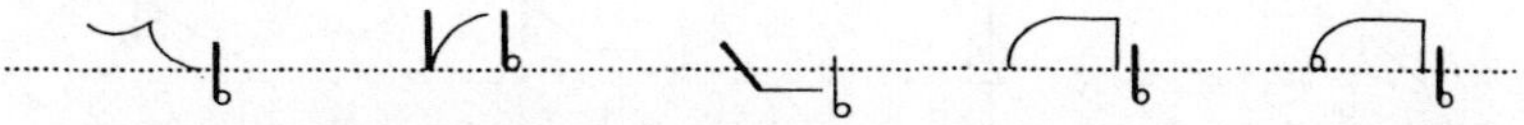

informed us delayed us booked us located us selected us

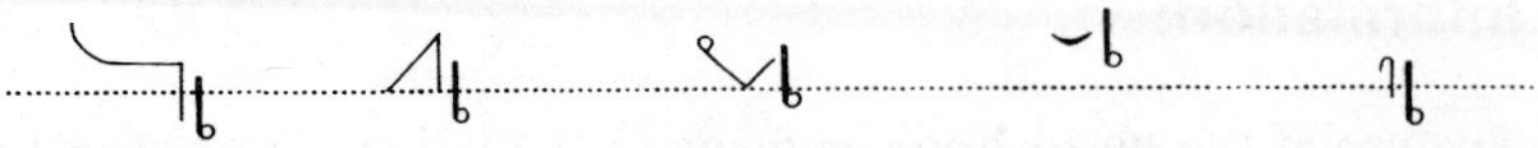

affected us rated us supported us handed us treated us

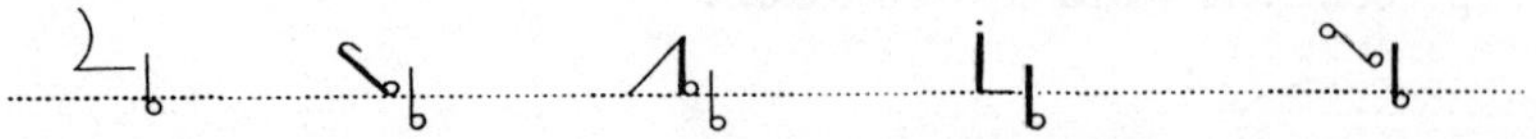

asked us blessed us reduced us conducted us surprised us

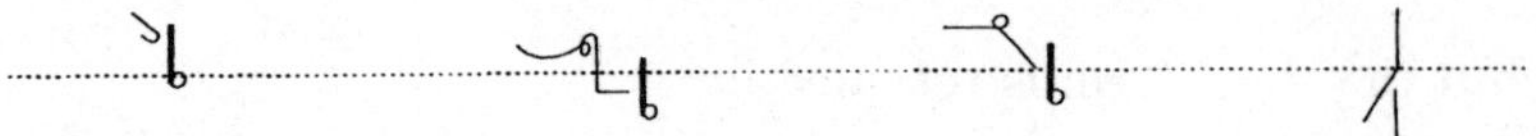

appointed us instructed us expected us touched us

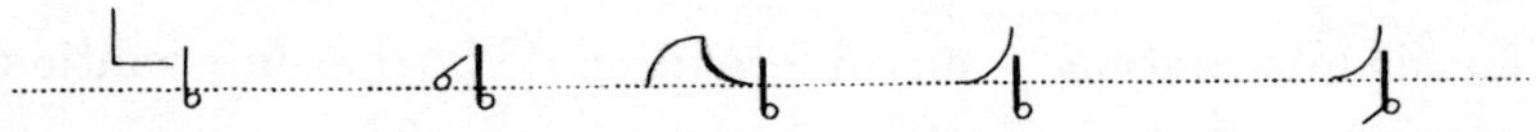

attacked us hated us loved us showed us showed us the

Hook **N** may be added to the disjoined **T** or **D** to represent the word **on** and tick **the** may be added to the hook:

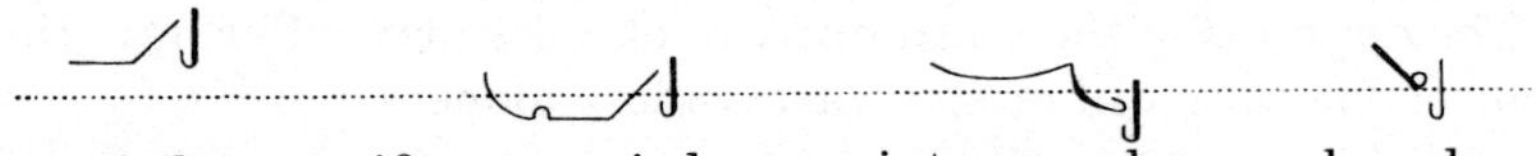

carried on if you carried on intervened on based on

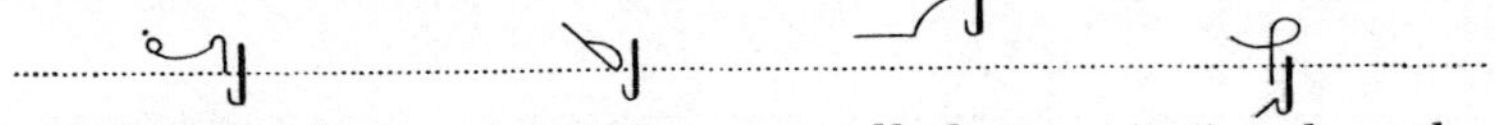

concentrated on pasted on called on insisted on the

The **OW** diphthong may be added to a half-length disjoined **T** or **D** to represent the word **out** and tick **the** may be added to the diphthong:

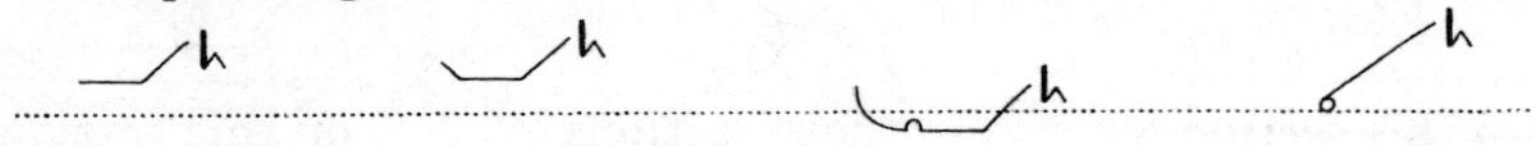

carried out I carried out if you carried out hurried out

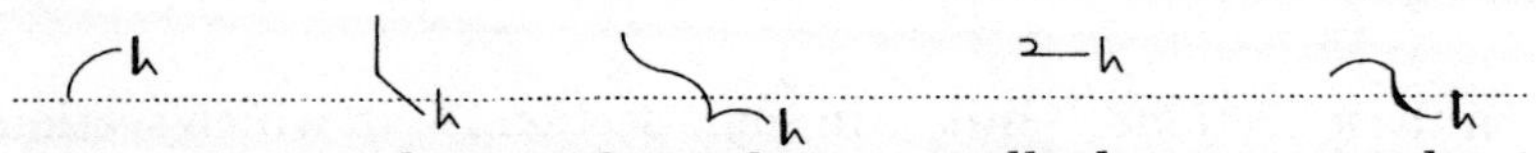

laid out typed out farmed out walked out moved out

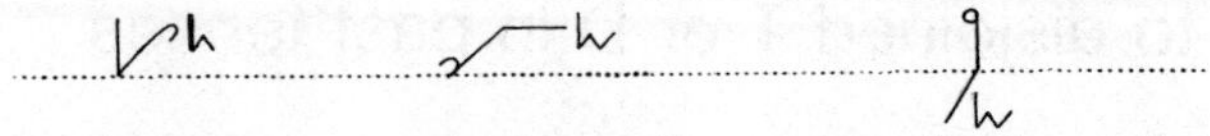

turned out worked out the stretched out the

Hook **F** may be added to a half-length disjoined **T** or **D** to represent the word **off** and tick **the** may be added to the hook:

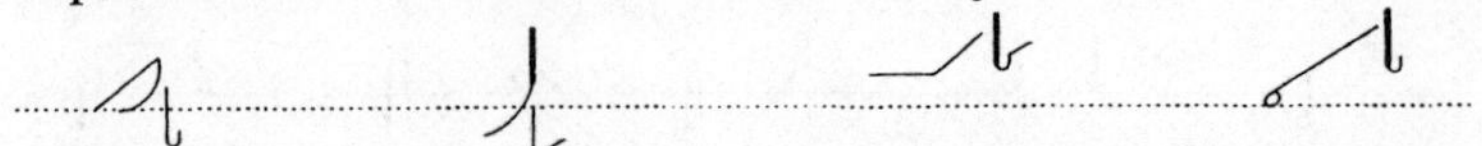

rushed off dashed off the carried off the hurried off

Intersections may also be written through a disjoined **T** or **D**:

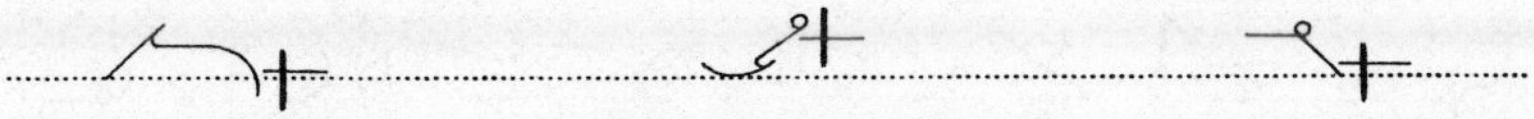

required capital | unused capital | expected capital

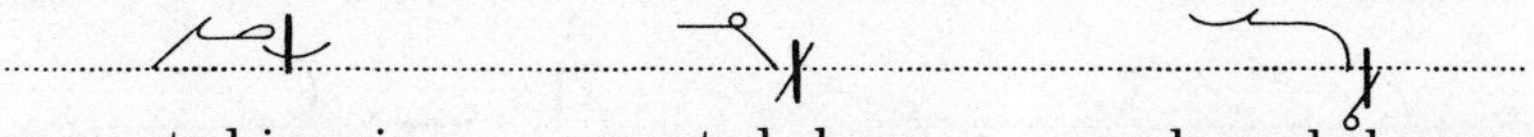

requested inquiry | expected charge | uncleared charges

expected requirements | anticipated requirements | expected business | related business

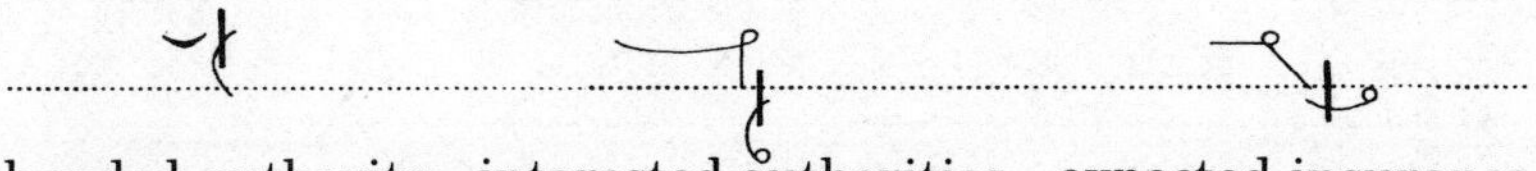

handed authority | interested authorities | expected insurance

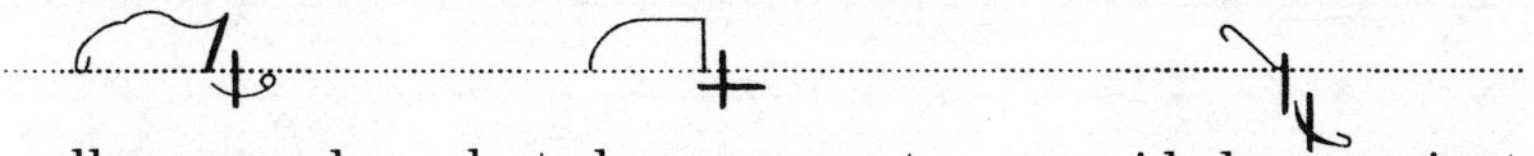

well-managed insurance | elected government | provided convenient

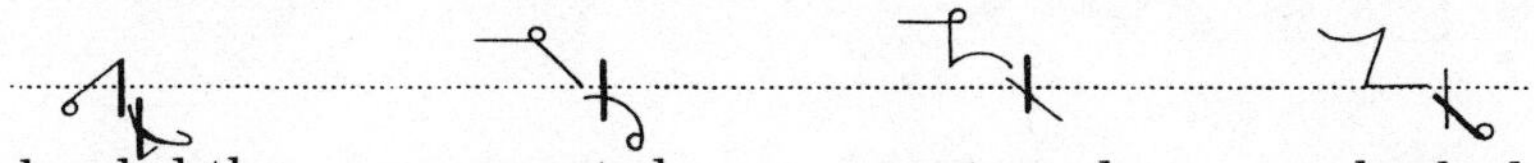

heeded the convenience | expected arrangements | accustomed policy | unchecked bills

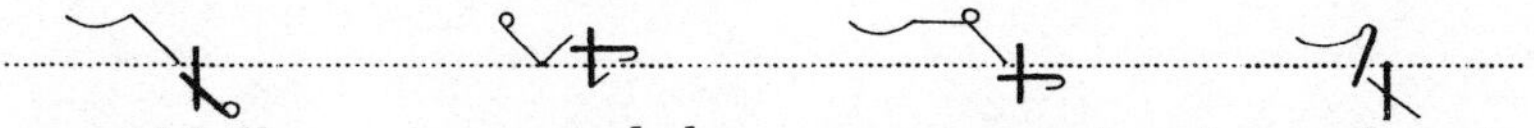

unpaid bills | supported the beginning | unexpected beginning | injured party

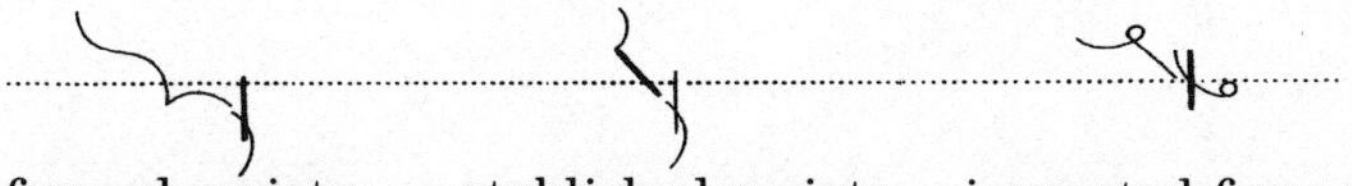

formed society | established society | inspected forms

Passage 16

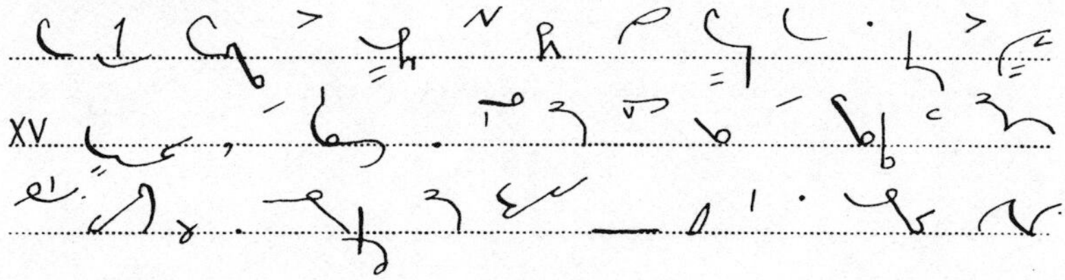

Unit Nine

Short Forms and Derivatives

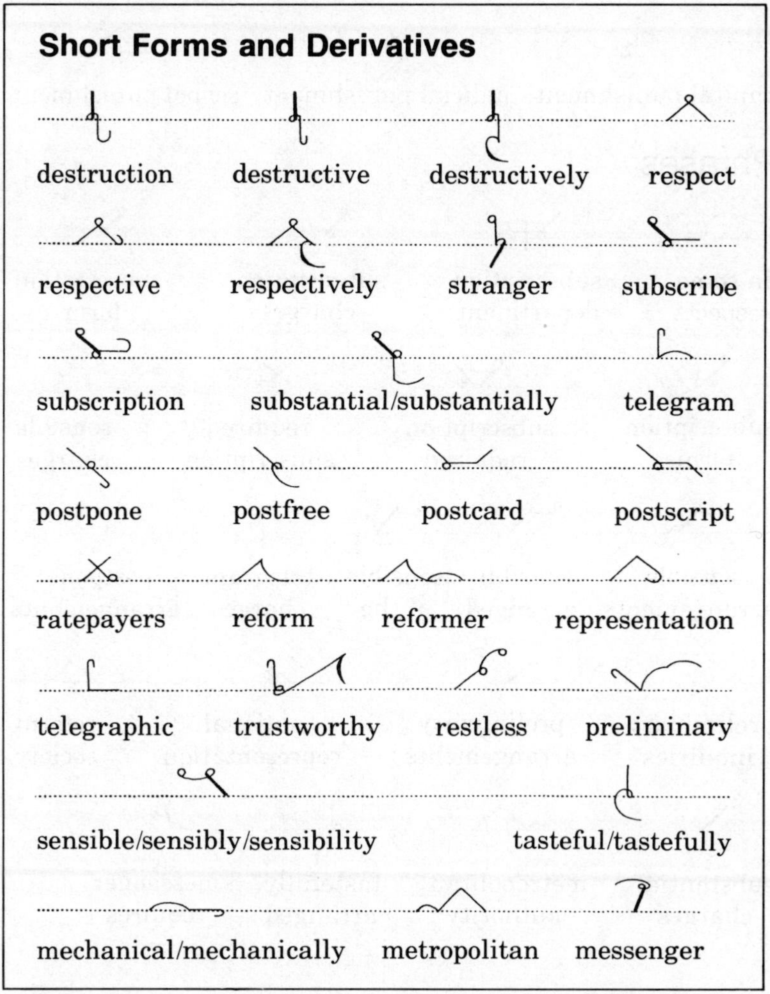

Note: The outline for the word **giant** is written  to distinguish it from **gentleman** 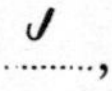, and the outline for the word **porter** is written 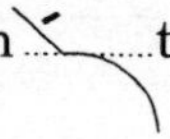 to distinguish it from **operator** 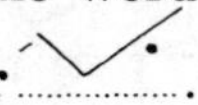.

Intersection

P, hook **N** may be intersected to represent the word **punishment:**

severe punishment | some punishment | your punishment

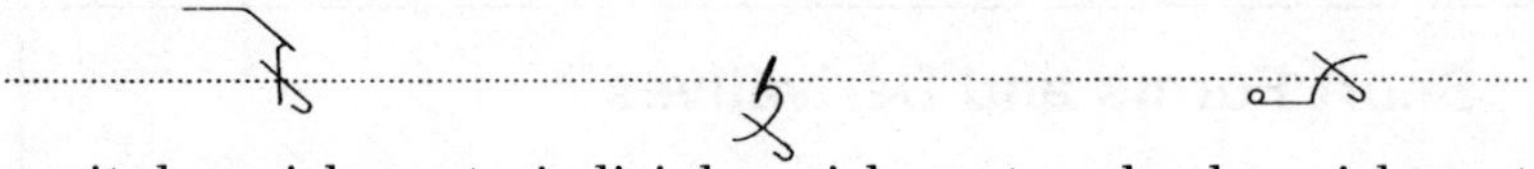

capital punishment | judicial punishment | school punishment

Phrases

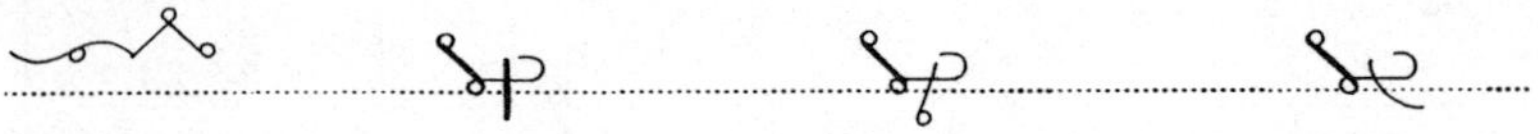

in some respects | subscription department | subscription charges | subscription form

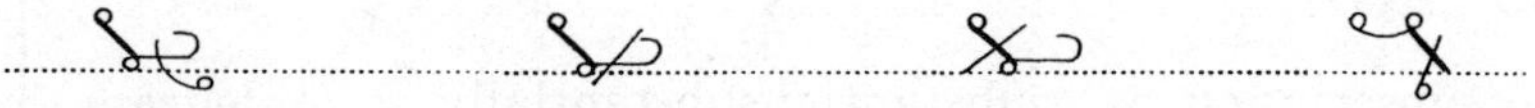

subscription forms | subscription required | required subscription | sensible charges

sensible arrangements | sensibly arranged | sensible of the | telegram charges | postpone arrangements

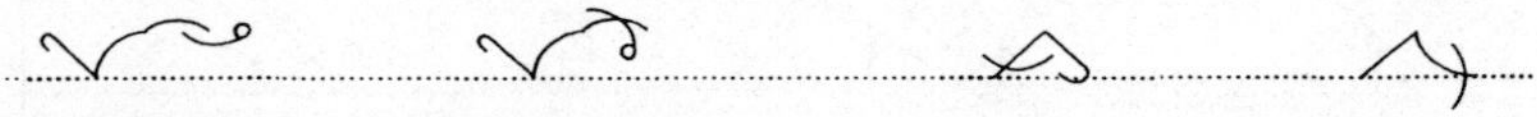

preliminary inquiries | preliminary arrangements | national representation | reform society

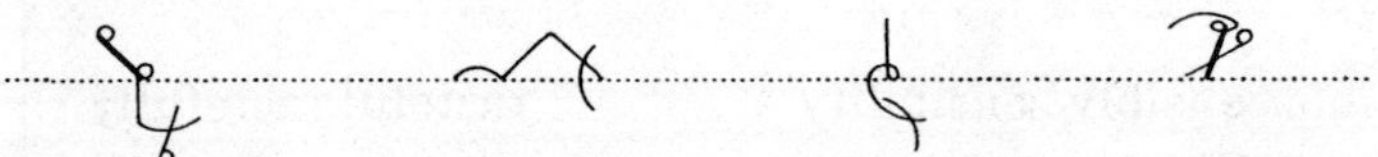

substantial charges | metropolitan authority | tastefully arranged | messenger requires

Passage 17

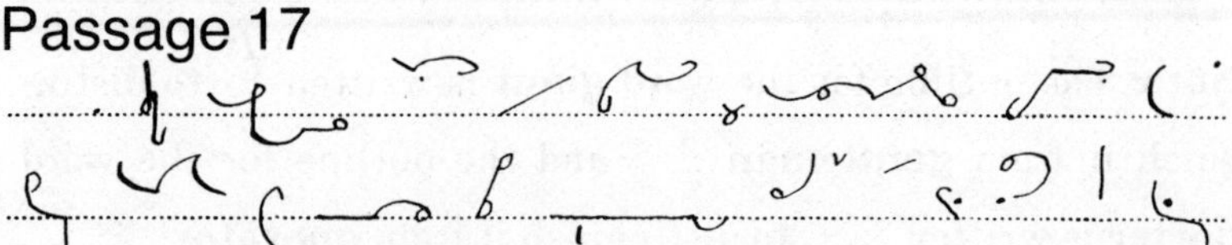

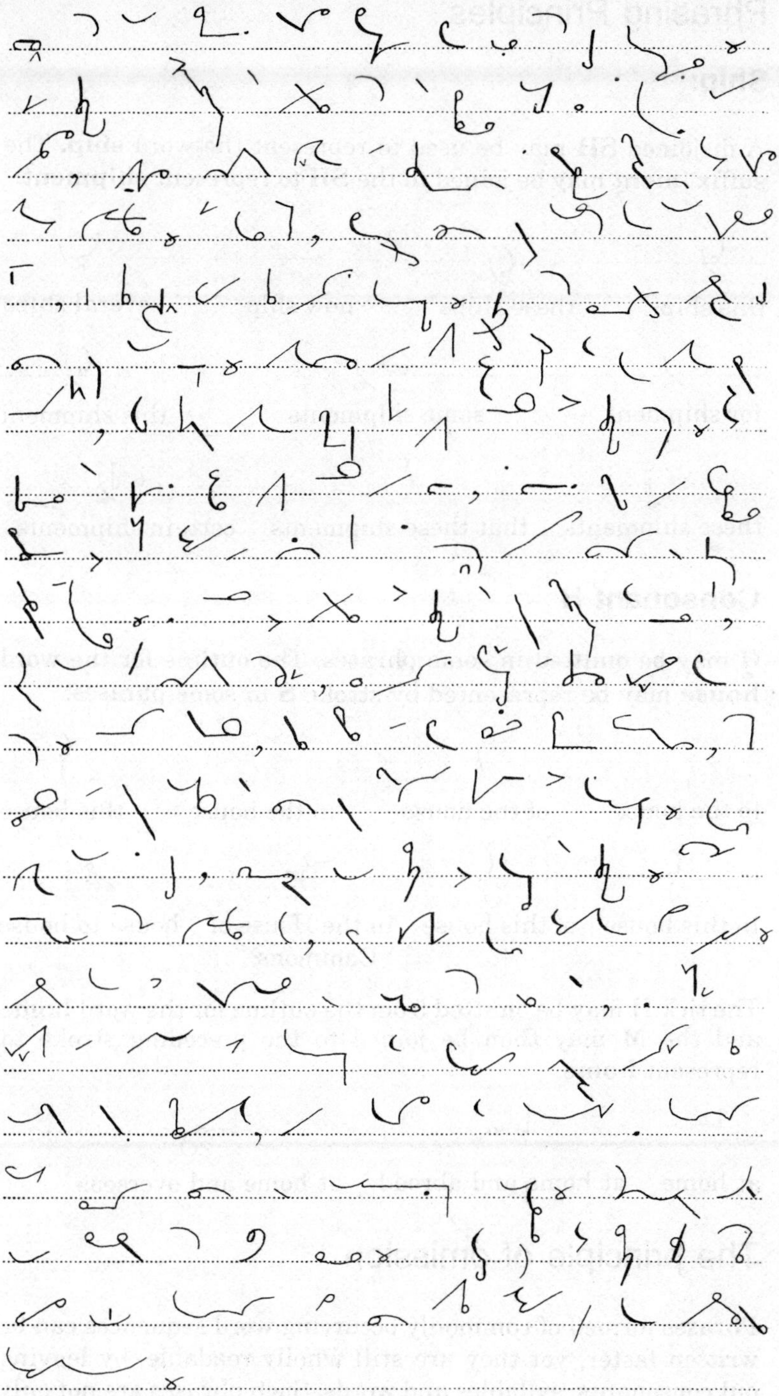

Phrasing Principles

Ship:

A disjoined **SH** may be used to represent the word **ship.** The suffix **-ment** may be joined to the **SH** to represent **shipment:**

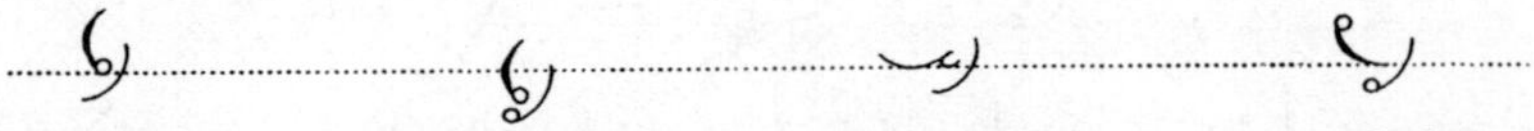

this ship these ships new ship several ships

for shipment some shipments this shipment

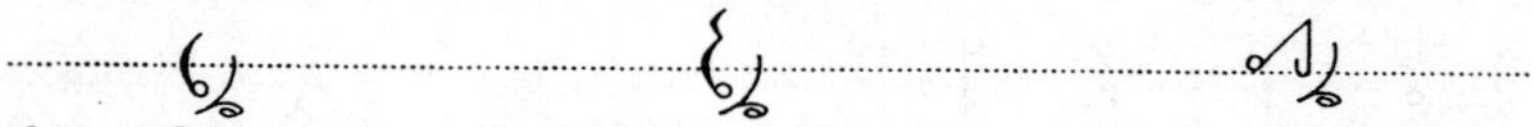

these shipments that these shipments certain shipments

Consonant H

H may be omitted in some phrases. The outline for the word **house** may be represented by stroke **S** in some phrases:

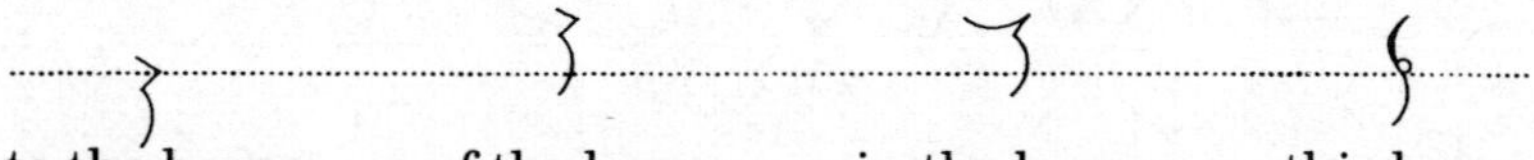

to the house of the house in the house this house

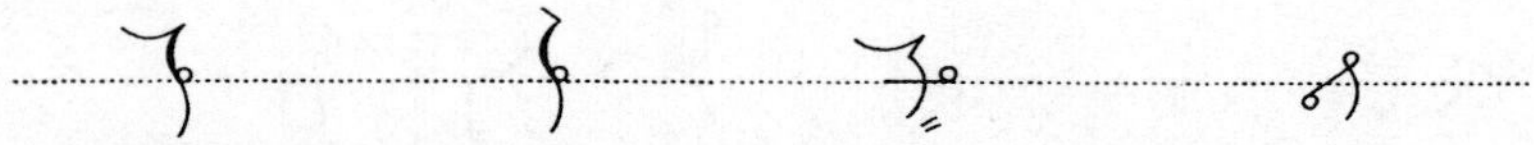

in this house of this house in the House of Commons house to house

The tick **H** may be omitted from the outline for the word **home** and the **M** may then be joined to the preceding stroke to represent **home**:

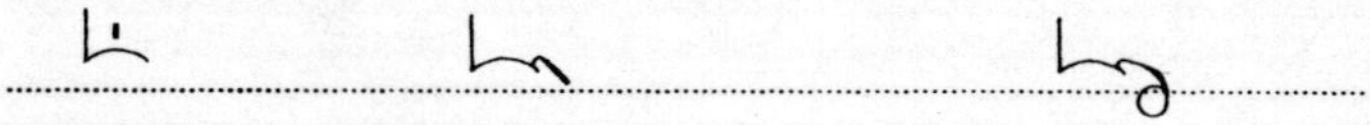

at home at home and abroad at home and overseas

The principle of omission

Phrases formed of commonly occurring word sequences can be written faster, yet they are still wholly readable, by leaving out consonants, syllables and words. Such phrases are not only very quick to write but they are also easy to transcribe. The following phrases show the omission of consonants, syllables and words. The omitted sections appear in parentheses:

Omission of consonant(s):

in other (r)espects 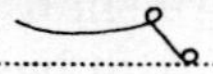

and in like (m)anner 

and in the same (m)anner 

towards o(n)e another 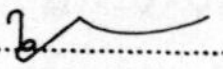

private sec(r)etary 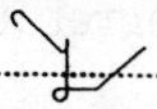

as (r)egards 

he has (r)eceived 

almos(t) certain 

mos(t) probably 

o(n)e another 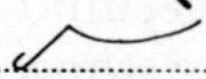

Home Sec(r)etary 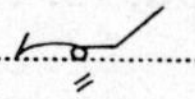

we have (r)eceived 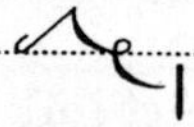

I have (r)eceived 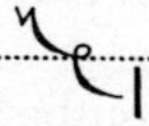

practical (ex)perience 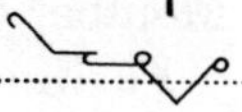

Omission of word(s):

thank you (for your) letter 

out (of) place 

expect (to) receive 

in (the) hands (of) 

ought (to) have 

ought (to) have known 

Mr. (and) Mrs. 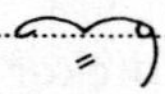

rates (and) taxes 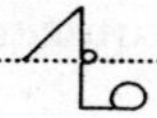

right (or) wrong 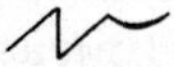

in (the) first instance 

freedom (of the) press 

difference (of) opinion 

differences (of) opinion 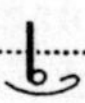

expression (of) opinion 

do you mean (to) say 

that is (to) say 

time (and) effort	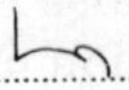	I am sorry (to) say	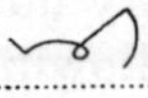
one (or) two		needless (to) say	
some (of) them	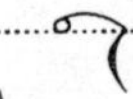	sign (of the) times	
five (or) six	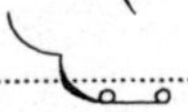	for (the) sake (of)	
facts (of the) case	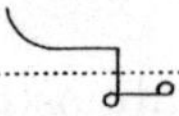	we shall be glad (to) hear	
seems (to) have		fact (of the) matter	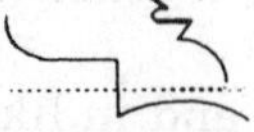
peculiar circum-stances (of the) case	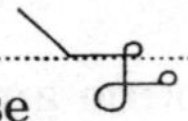	facts (of the) matter	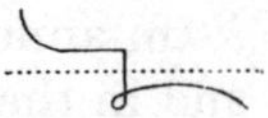
out (of the) question	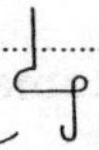	over (and) above	
yes (or) no	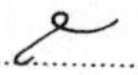	regret (to) state	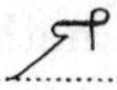
Act (of) Parliament	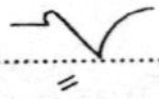	Acts (of) Parliament	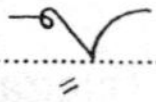
Member (of) Parliament		Members (of) Parliament	

Omission of word(s) and consonant(s):

in (a) great (m)easure		to (a) great (ex)tent	
in (the) las(t) place	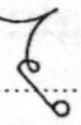	notwithstanding (the) (f)act	
in (point of) (f)act		nor(th) (and) south	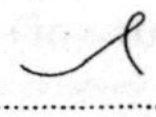
in such (a) (m)anner as	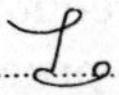	in (r)espect (to)	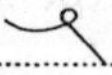
in (the) nex(t) place	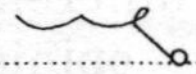	we shall be glad (to) (r)eceive	
with (r)ef(eren)ce (to) which	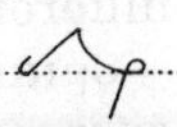	wi(th) (r)espect (to)	
wi(th) (r)egard (to)	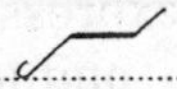	in (r)egard (to)	
near(er) (and) nearer		qui(cker) (and) quicker	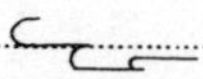

Omission of a syllable:

Omission of **-hand**:

short(hand) writer		short(hand) writing	

Omission of **in**:

if you will (in)struct		I am (in)structed	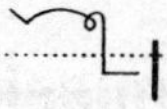
we are (in)structed	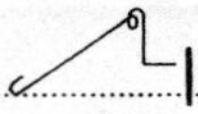	will be (in)structed	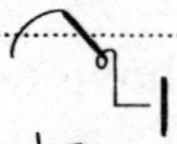
he will be (in)structed	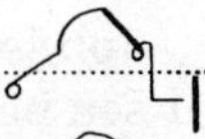	she will be (in)structed	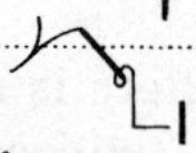
we were (in)structed	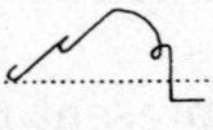	to be (in)structed	
that we have to be (in)structed	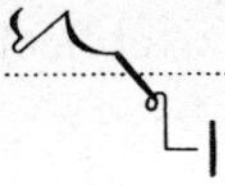	musical (in)strument	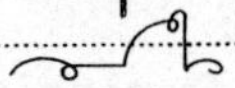

Omission of -ly:

extreme(ly) sorry	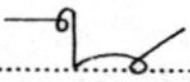	extreme(ly) regret	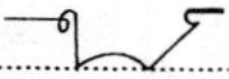
extreme(ly) regrettable	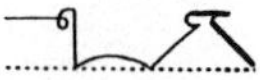	distinct(ly) understood	

Omission of -ish:

Brit(ish) Museum		Brit(ish) Isles	
Brit(ish) manufacture	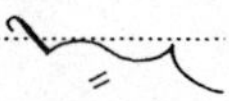	Brit(ish) manufacturers	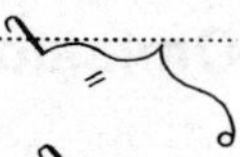
Brit(ish) people		Brit(ish) custom	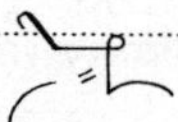
Brit(ish) customs		Brit(ish) Rail	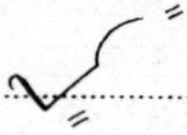
Brit(ish) association		Brit(ish) production	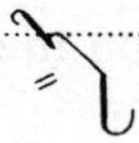

Omission of -nical:

tech(nical) college		tech(nical) colleges	
tech(nical) difficulty	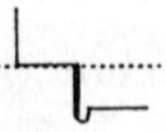	tech(nical) difficulties	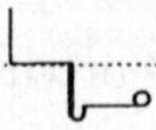
tech(nical) terms	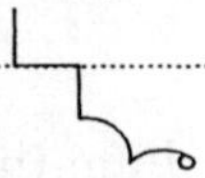	tech(nical) progress	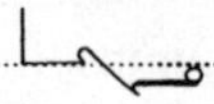

Omission of ob-:

I have no (ob)jection	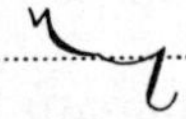	we have no (ob)jection	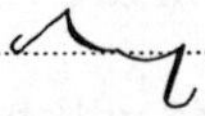
there is no (ob)jection		I see no (ob)jection	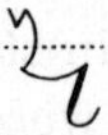
I take no (ob)jection		present no (ob)jection	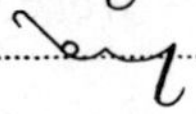

Omission of pre-:

high (pre)ssure		low (pre)ssure	
water (pre)ssure		extreme (pre)ssure	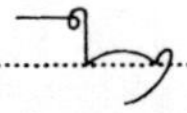
too much (pre)ssure		steam (pre)ssure	
inflationary (pre)ssures		blood (pre)ssure	

Omission of word(s), consonant(s) and syllable(s):

in (r)ef(eren)ce (to) which	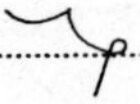	wi(th) (r)ef(eren)ce (to)	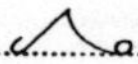
in (the) th(ird) place	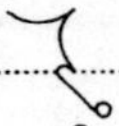	in (r)ef(eren)ce (to)	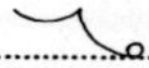
ex(traordinary) g(eneral) m(eet)ing	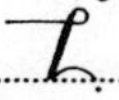	ann(ual) g(eneral) meeting	

Omission of a vowel:

it may (a)lso		it may (a)lso be	
it is (a)lso		you may (a)lso	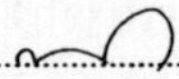
you may (a)lso be	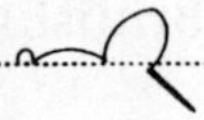	it will (a)lso be	

Passage 18

Unit Ten

Short Forms and Derivatives

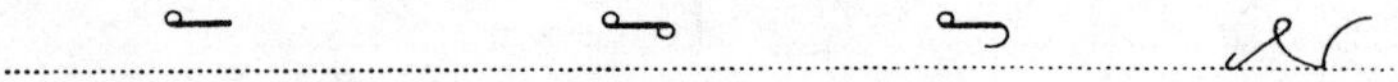

significant/signify significance signification wasteful

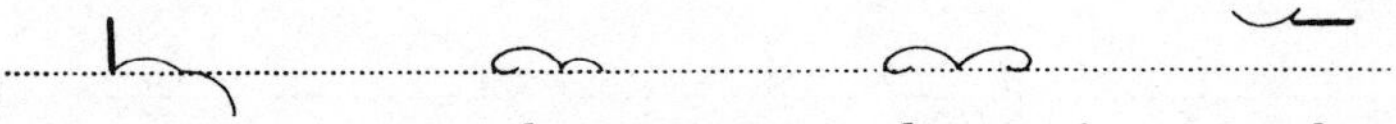

administrator amalgamate amalgamation neglect

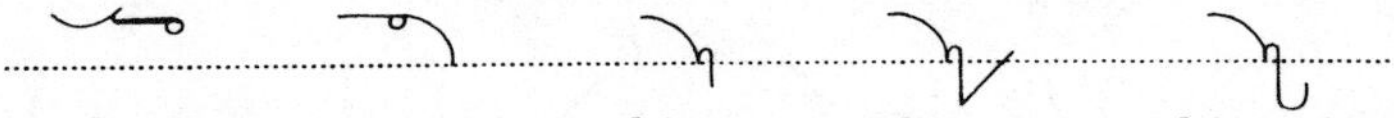

negligence executor arbitrate arbitary arbitration

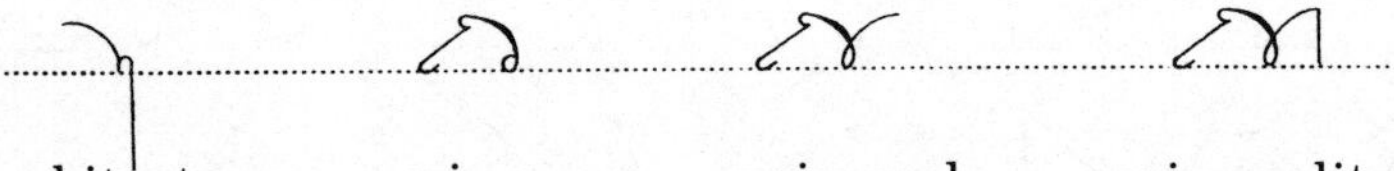

arbitrator universe universal universality

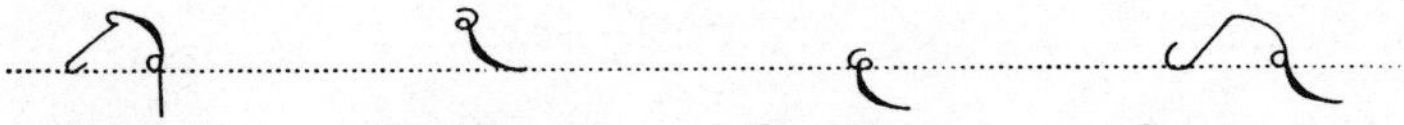

university whatsoever whensoever wheresoever

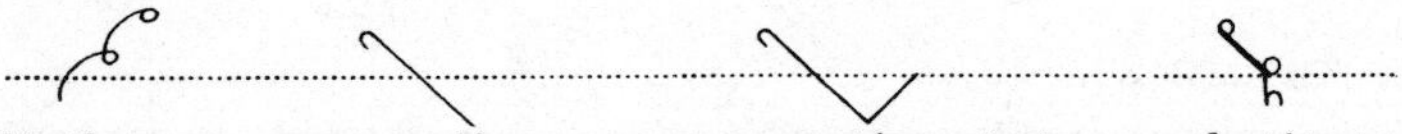

listless proportion proportionate/proportionately substitute

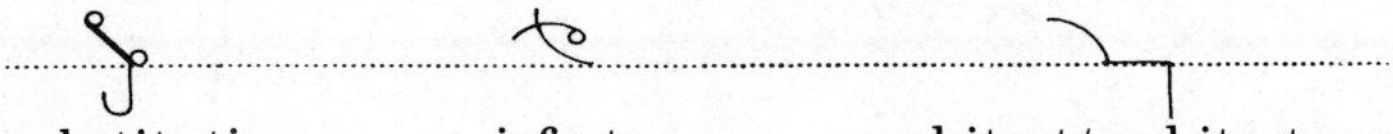

substitution misfortune architect/architecture/architectural

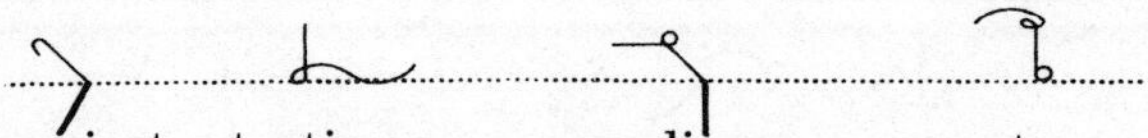

project testimony expediency monstrous

Note: The outline for the word **antithesis** is written .... to distinguish it from **analysis** ...., and the outline for the word **heroine** is written .... to distinguish it from **hunter** ....

Intersection

Stroke **V** may be intersected to represent the word **valuation:**

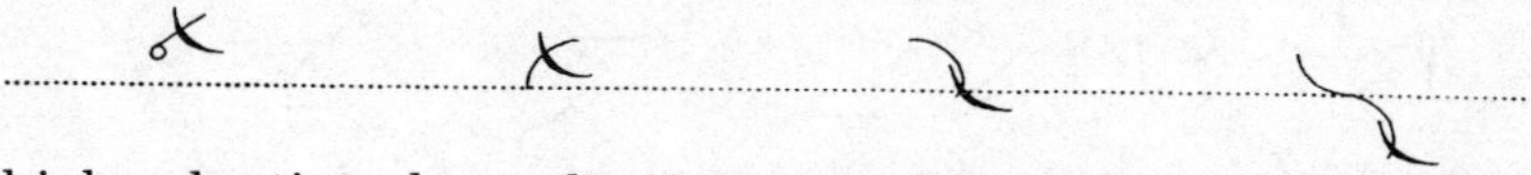

high valuation | low valuation | your valuation | fair valuation

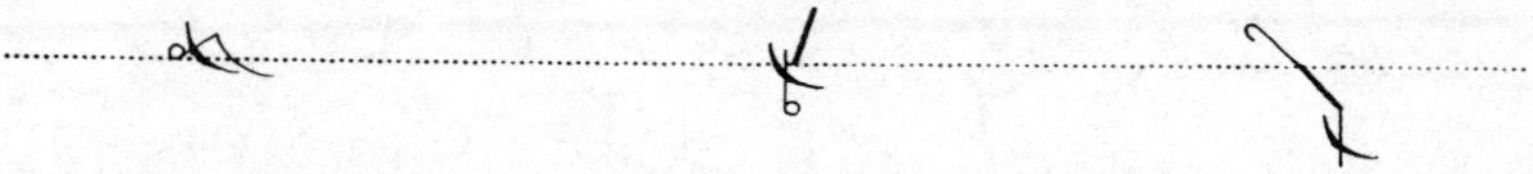

valuation certificate | agent's valuation | probate valuation

our valuation | their valuation | incorrect valuation

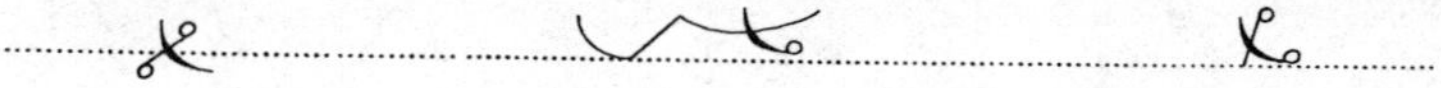

house valuation | furniture valuations | such valuations

P, hook **L** may be intersected to represent the word **application:**

this application | my application | your application

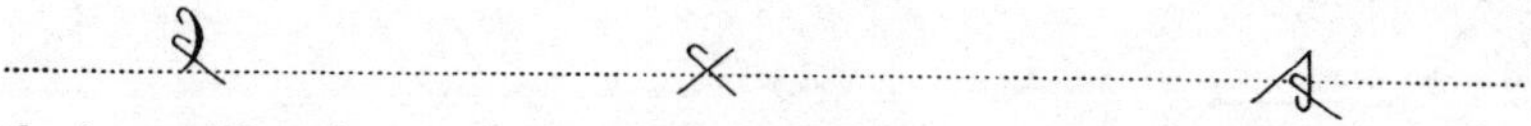

their application | our application | written application

formal application | make application | to make application

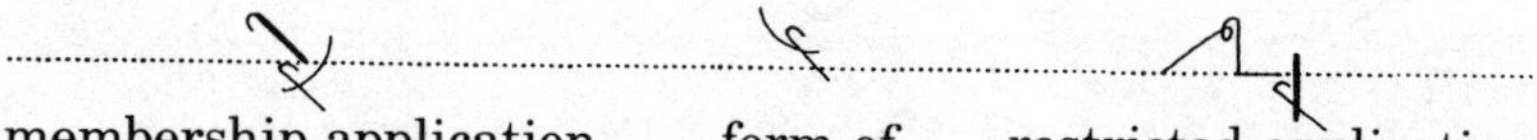

membership application | form of application | restricted application

Passage 19

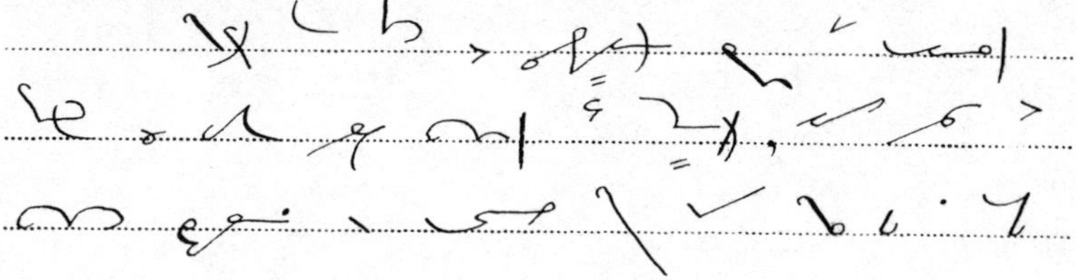

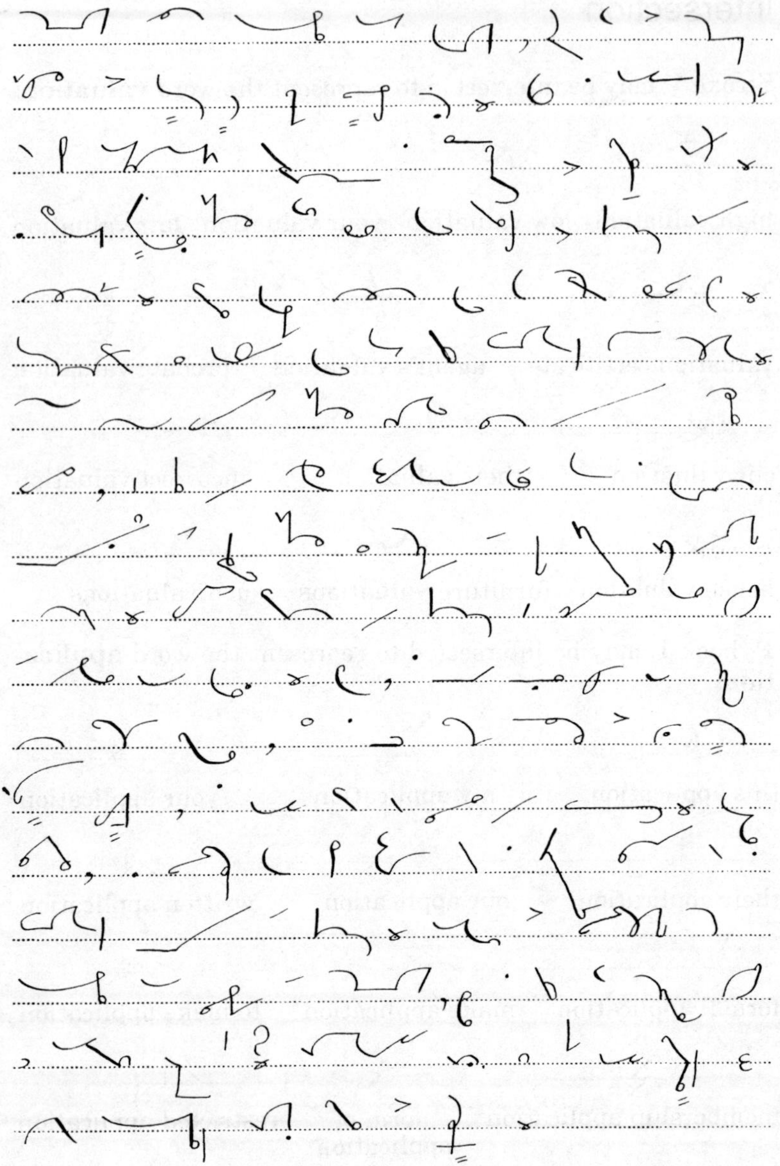

Phrasing Principles

In order to produce an exact transcription from shorthand notes, it is necessary to insert a vowel in some phrases and/or to change the position of an outline or to write an outline in full in order to distinguish the formal from the colloquial.

I am	I'm
you are	you're
we are	we're
he is	he's
she is	she's
that is	that's
I will	I'll
you will	you'll
he will	he'll
she will	she'll
they will	they'll
it will	it'll
I would	I'd
they would	they'd
I have	I've
you have	you've
they have	they've
I cannot	I can't
you cannot	you can't

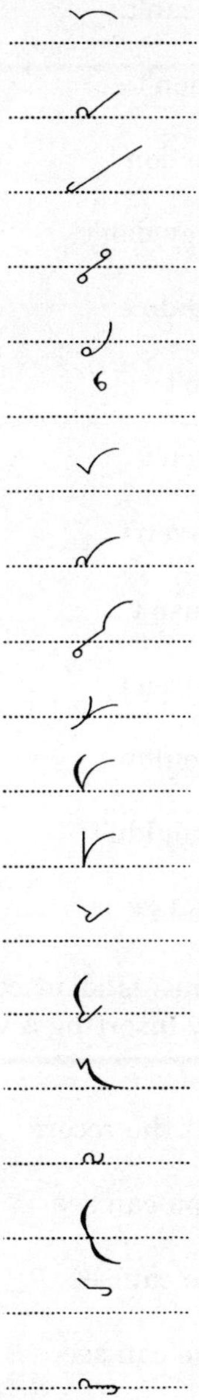

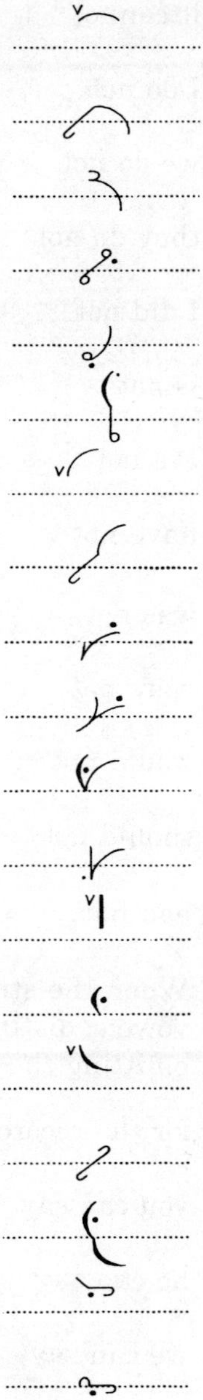

he cannot	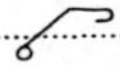	he can't	
she cannot		she can't	
we cannot	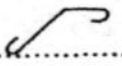	we can't	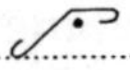
it cannot		it can't	
I do not		I don't	
we do not		we don't	
they do not		they don't	
I did not		I didn't	
is not		isn't	
are not	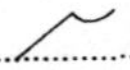	aren't	
have not		haven't	
was not		wasn't	
were not		weren't	
would not		wouldn't	
should not		shouldn't	
had not		hadn't	

When the structure of two outlines is identical except for the vowels, distinction is obtained by inserting a vowel in one and omitting the vowel in the other:

for the record		off the record	
you can say	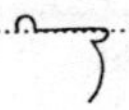	you can see	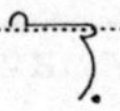
he can say	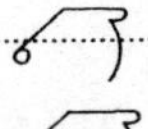	he can see	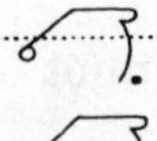
we can say	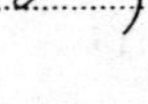	we can see	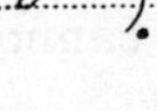

I give  I gave 

we give 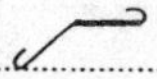 we gave 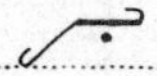

young man  young men 

Evening

When the word **evening** occurs after any day of the week, it may be represented by a hook **V** and a dot **ing**:

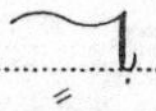 Monday evening 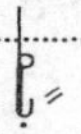 Tuesday evening 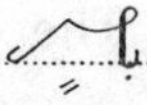 Wednesday evening

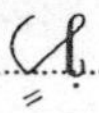 Thursday evening  Friday evening  Saturday evening

 Sunday evening

This high speed device may also be used after the short form **yesterday**:

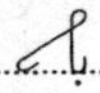 yesterday evening

The disjoined dash for the suffix **ings** may also be used:

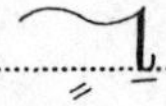 Monday evenings 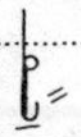 Tuesday evenings 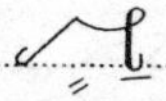 Wednesday evenings

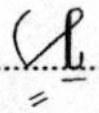 Thursday evenings 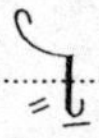 Friday evenings 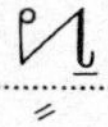 Saturday evenings

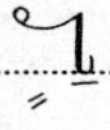 Sunday evenings

The full outline for **evening** is used in the following:

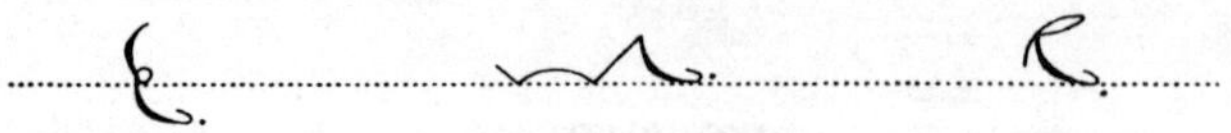

this evening   tomorrow evening   last evening

Effect

A useful phrase to learn is:

into effect

Note: The outline for the word **marital** is written to distinguish it from **mortal** , and the outline for the word **sacred** is written to distinguish it from **secret** .

Passage 20

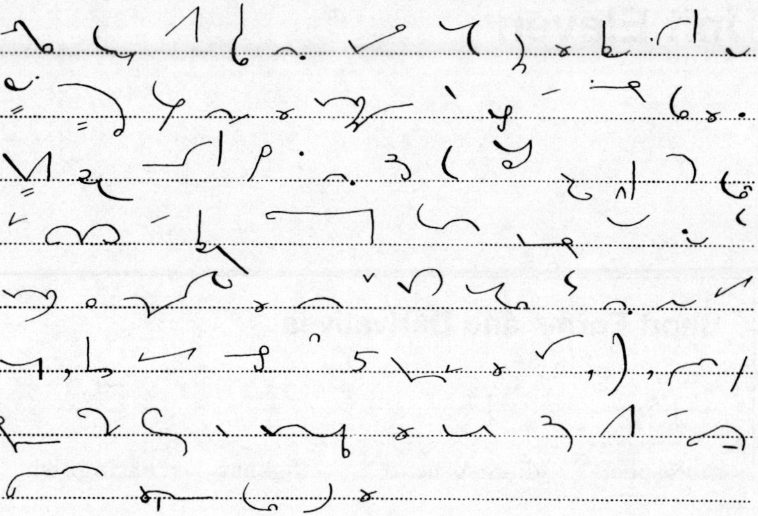

Unit Eleven

Short Forms and Derivatives

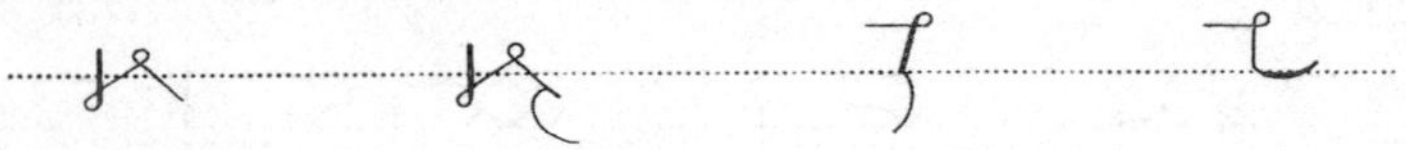

disrespect | disrespectful | exigency | extinguish

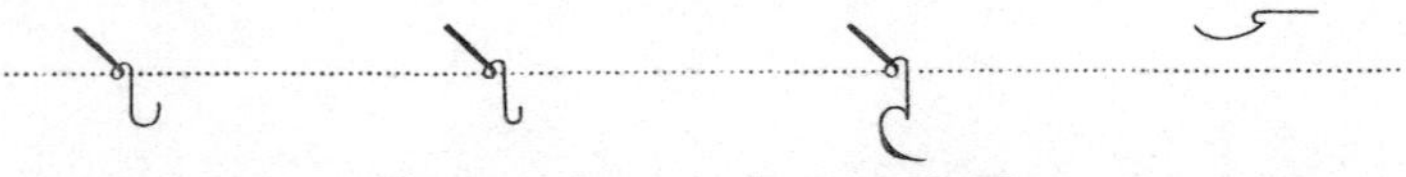

obstruction | obstructive | obstructively | incorporate

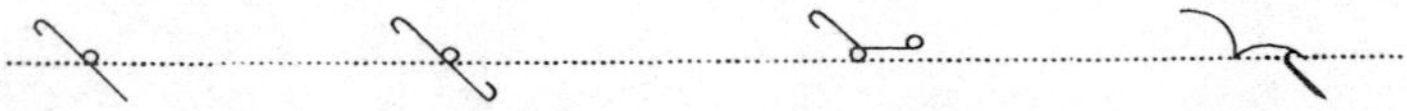

prospect | prospective | prospectus | removable

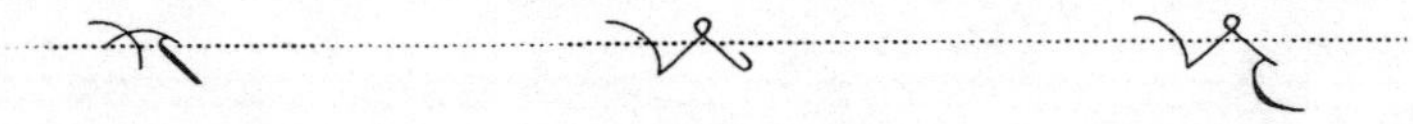

irremovable | irrespective | irrespectively

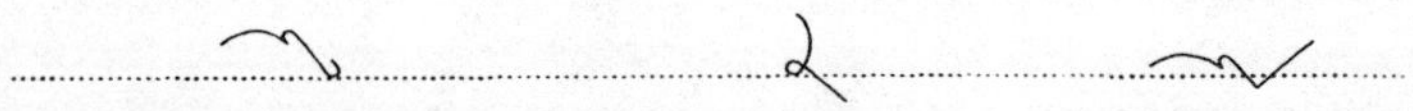

imperfect/imperfection/imperfectly | suspect | imperturbable

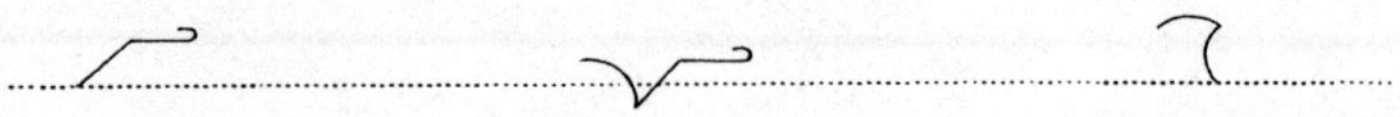

recoverable | irrecoverable/irrecoverably | mathematical/mathematically

Short Forms and Derivatives

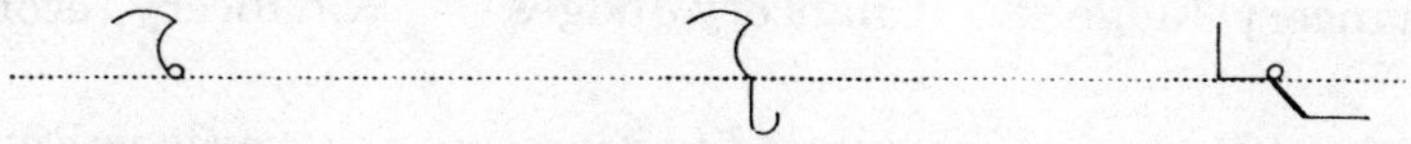

mathematics — mathematician — textbook

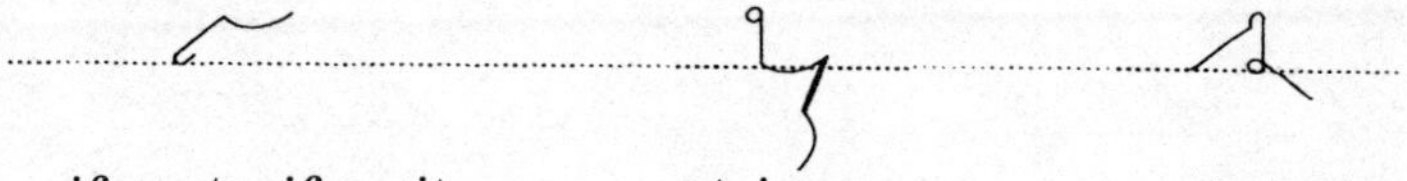

uniform/uniformity uniformly — stringency — retrospect

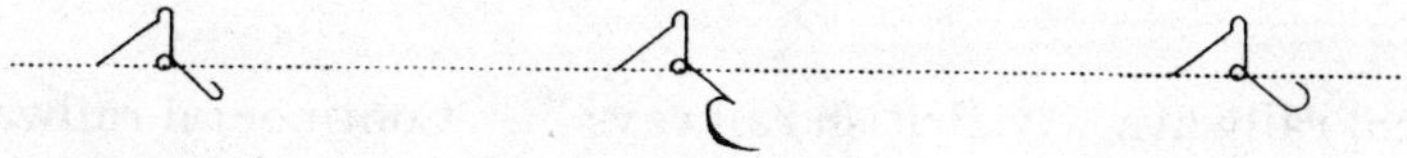

retrospective — retrospectively — retrospection

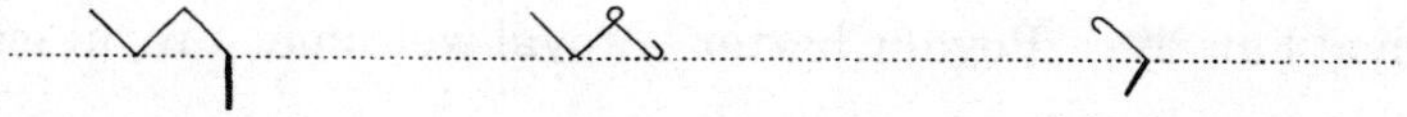

perpendicular — perspective — prejudice/prejudicial prejudicially

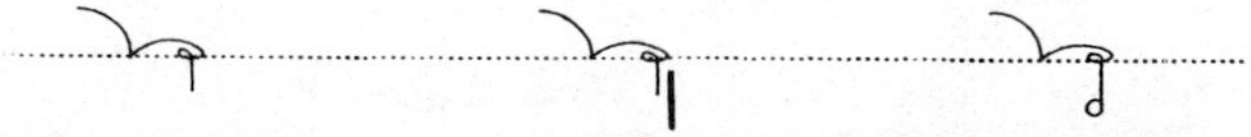

remonstrate — remonstrated — remonstrance

Note: The outline for the word **secretariat** is written to distinguish it from **secretary**, and the outline for the word **resuscitate** is written to distinguish it from **resist**.

Intersection

CH may be intersected to represent the word **chancery:**

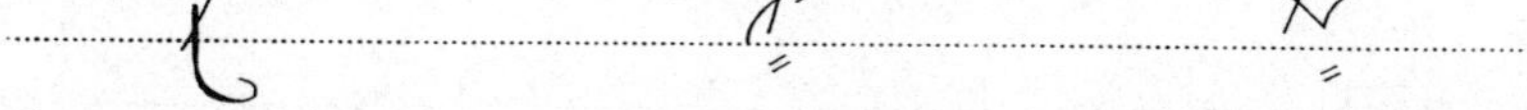

chancery division — Chancery Lane — Chancery Appeal

Chancery Judge Chancery Judges Chancery records

Upward **R** may be intersected to represent the words **railway** and **royal**. Circle **S** may be added to the upward **R** to represent **railways:**

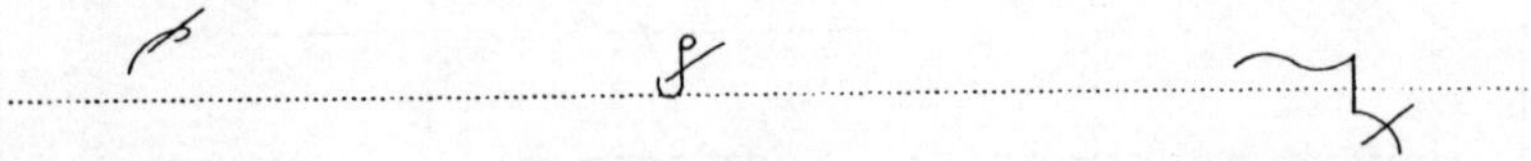

railway line railway station miniature railway

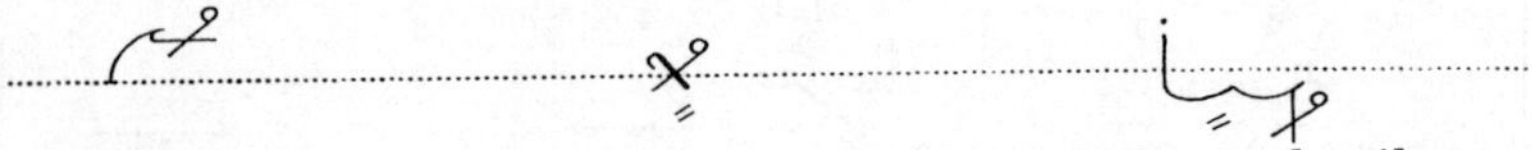

local railways British railways Continental railways

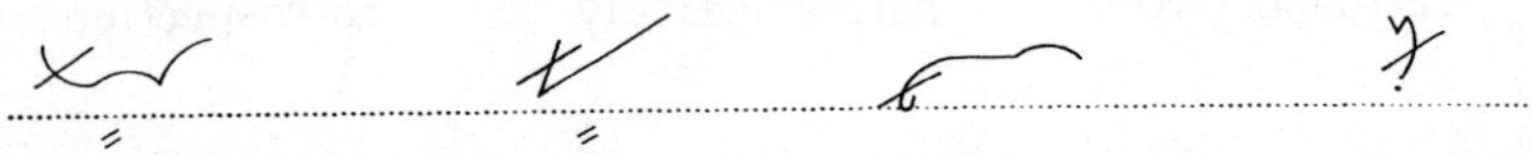

Royal Family Royal Charter royal welcome royal icing

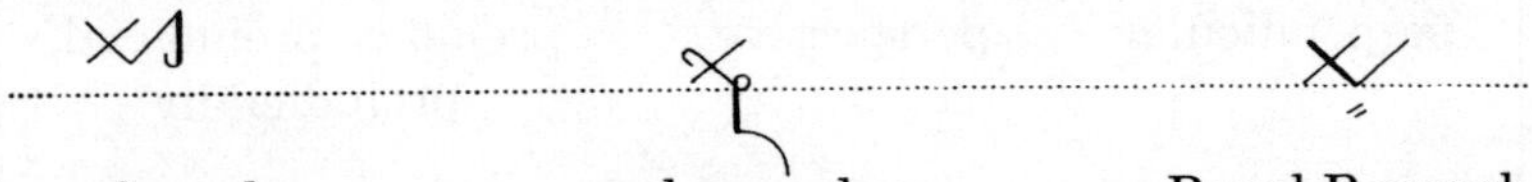

royal pardon royal procedure Royal Borough

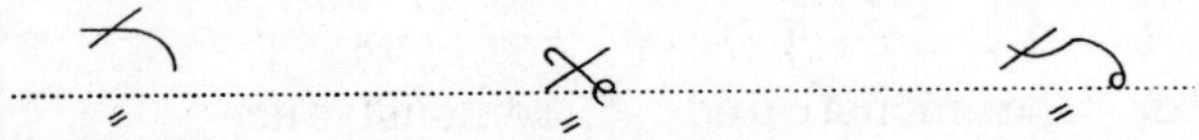

Royal Car Royal procession Royal nurse

Passage 21

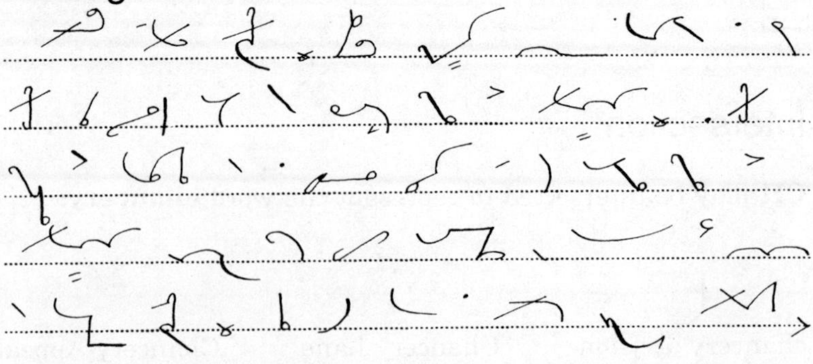

Figures

A useful device to represent **thousand** is a long oblique line (preferably written upwards). Although it is not possible to join this to a preceding outline or to figures, it can be written very quickly:

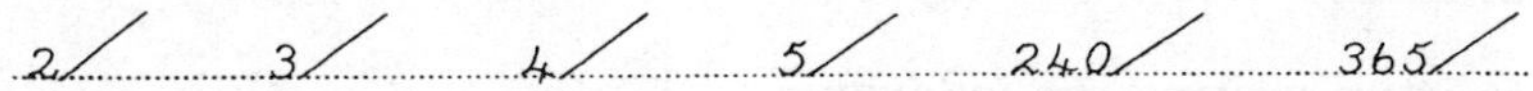

2,000 3,000 4,000 5,000 240,000 365,000

The preceding device may be used for amounts of money if a dot representing pounds is added after the oblique stroke:

£2,000 £4,000 £7,000 £8,000 £321,000 £928,000

Although these abbreviating devices are somewhat unorthodox, they are useful short cuts.

Dates

The oblique line suggested for **thousand** may also be used to represent the present century in dates:

1979 /79   1980 /80   1981 /81

However, when reference is made to previous or forthcoming centuries, the year must be written in full:

1867 1867   1888 1888   2004 2004

Fractions

The three most common fractions $\frac{1}{4}$, $\frac{1}{2}$ and $\frac{3}{4}$ may be represented in the following way:
The $\frac{1}{4}$ is a horizontal stroke containing an initial tick, written above the figure as in:

$2\frac{1}{4}$ 2 $4\frac{1}{4}$ 4

The $\frac{1}{2}$ is a horizontal stroke written above the figure, as in:

$3\frac{1}{2}$ $\overline{3}$ $6\frac{1}{2}$ $\overline{6}$

The $\frac{3}{4}$ is a horizontal stroke with a final tick, written above the figure as in:

$2\frac{3}{4}$ 2 $7\frac{3}{4}$ 7

Practise writing the following:

$4\frac{1}{4}$ 4 $4\frac{1}{2}$ $\overline{4}$ $4\frac{3}{4}$ 4

$5\frac{1}{4}$ 5 $5\frac{1}{2}$ $\overline{5}$ $5\frac{3}{4}$ 5

$7\frac{1}{4}$ 7 $7\frac{1}{2}$ $\overline{7}$ $7\frac{3}{4}$ 7

The signs representing these three fractions may also be used in conjunction with **P** representing **per cent:**

4 per cent 4\ $4\frac{1}{2}$ per cent 4\

5 per cent 5\ $5\frac{1}{2}$ per cent 5\

6 per cent	$6\frac{1}{2}$ per cent
$4\frac{1}{4}$ per cent	$4\frac{3}{4}$ per cent
$5\frac{1}{4}$ per cent	$5\frac{3}{4}$ per cent
$6\frac{1}{4}$ per cent	$6\frac{3}{4}$ per cent

When the phrase **per cent per annum** occurs, **P** may be repeated to represent **per annum:**

4 per cent	4 per cent per annum
6 per cent	6 per cent per annum
$3\frac{1}{2}$ per cent	$3\frac{1}{2}$ per cent per annum
$7\frac{1}{4}$ per cent	$7\frac{1}{4}$ per cent per annum
$8\frac{3}{4}$ per cent	$8\frac{3}{4}$ per cent per annum

Monetary Units

Monetary units may be expressed in the following way:

francs Deutschmarks Swiss francs Lire French francs

Practise writing the following:

9 French francs	5 Deutschmarks	10 Swiss francs
1650 lire	10.4 francs	5.07 Deutschmarks
10.81 Swiss francs	1700 lire	1,000,000 lire

Scottish, Welsh and Irish consonants and vowels

The Scottish guttural **CH**, and the Irish **GH** are written: **Ch** .... , as in:

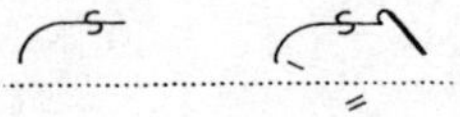

loch Lochaber

The Welsh **ll** by .... , as in:

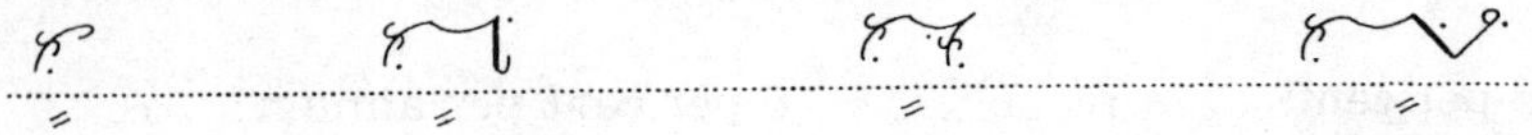

Llan Landaff Llanelly Llanberis

Foreign consonants and vowels

The German guttural **CH** is written .... , as in:

ich Dach

The French nasal **N** .... , as in:

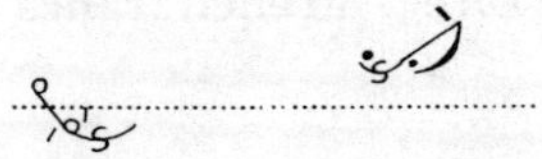

soupcon entourage

Two similar French and German vowels are represented in the following way:

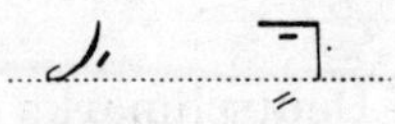

jeune Goethe

Note: The outline for the word **veritable** is written .... to distinguish it from **variable** ....

Intersections

J may be intersected to represent the word **journal:**

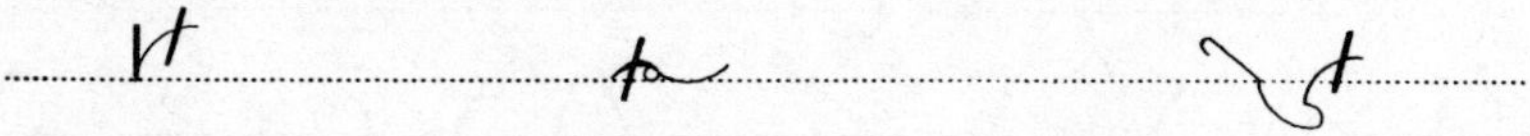

daily journal | journal of medicine | professional journal

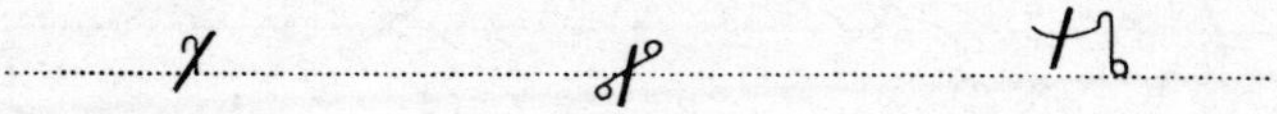

trade journal | house journal | journal entries

K, hook **R** may be intersected to represent the word **colonel:**

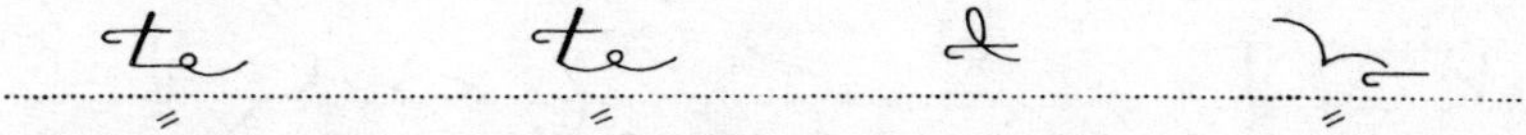

Colonel Jackson | Colonel Johnson | staff colonel | Army colonel

Circle **S** written on the hook **R** side of **P** may be intersected to represent the word **superintendent:**

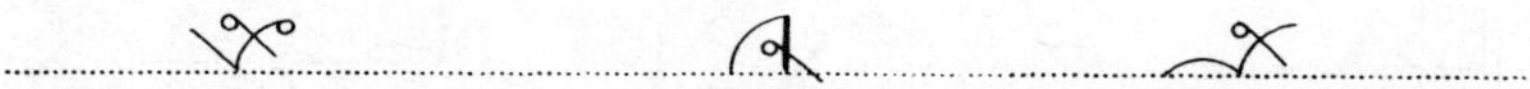

police superintendent | lady superintendent | male superintendent

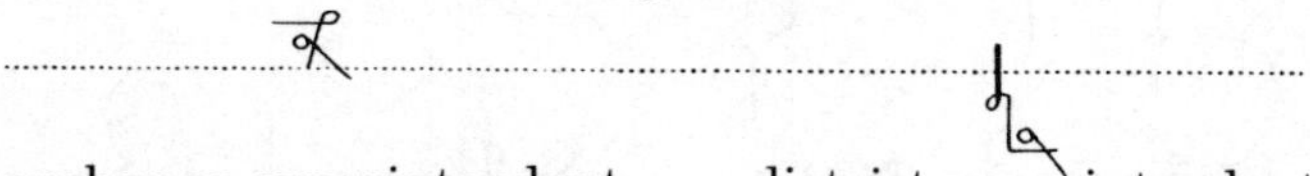

exchange superintendent | district superintendent

SH, circle **S** may be intersected to represent the word **assurance:**

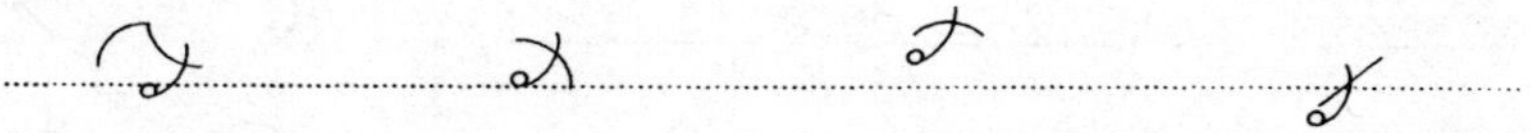

life assurance | your assurance | my assurance | our assurance

undoubted assurance | definite assurance | have my assurance

Passage 22

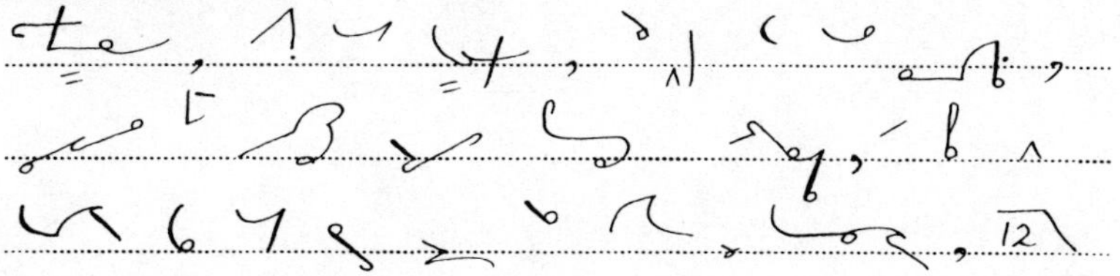

Unit Twelve

Throughout this text advanced principles of phrasing have been introduced but there must be an intelligent application of the various devices to meet the needs of the individual shorthand writer. Experienced shorthand writers will be able to devise their own phrases. This must not be done in a haphazard way but carried out with a great deal of thought. The phrases must be able to be written quickly and transcribed speedily and accurately. If a phrase can easily be misread, it should not be used.

The fields of interest that provide the phrases shown in this Unit – commerce, banking, government and political, legal – are those that cater for the needs of most verbatim shorthand writers. It is not necessary to read, drill, and practise these phrases since they are specialist in their application.

Commerce

account sales 

additional cost 

additional expense 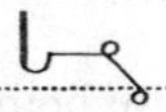

annual general meeting 

annual report 

at your earliest convenience 

board of directors 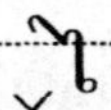

by return post 

by return of post

chairman said 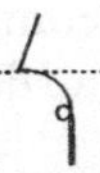

cumulative preference shares 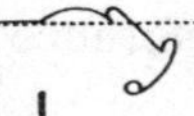

debenture stock 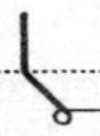

declaration of a dividend 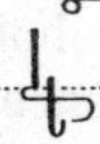

declare a dividend 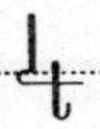

director's report 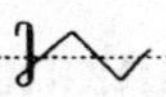

discount for cash 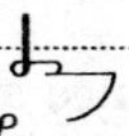

extraordinary general meeting 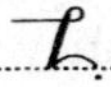

I am glad to move the adoption 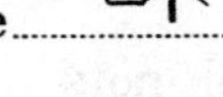

I have received your letter
industrial relations
in moving the adoption of the report and accounts
in reply to your letter
in your reply to my letter
interim dividend
managing director
monthly report
of the board
ordinary dividend
ordinary shareholders
paid up capital
paid up capital of the company
postal order
preference dividend
preference shareholders
preference shares
profit and loss account
profit margin
referring to your letter
registered letter
subsidiary companies
turn to the balance sheet
turning to the balance sheet
turning to the profit and loss account
value added tax
volume of business
we have received your letter
we shall be glad if you will
we thank you for your letter
will you kindly let me know
with best wishes
your board
your directors

Banking

advance against a life policy
bank giro
bank note
base rate
bearer cheque
cancel the cheque

cash dispenser

certified cheque

cheque card

clearing house

crossed cheque

direct debit

Executor and Trustee Department

giro credit

investment management service

joint stock bank

last indorser

negotiable instrument

negotiable security

not negotiable cheque

paying-in slip

rate of exchange

refer to drawer

restrictive indorsement

specially indorsed

standing order

travellers' cheques

Treasury bills

without recourse

written authority of the drawer

Government and Political

Act of Parliament

Agriculture, Fisheries and Food

at the first reading

at the second reading

at the third reading

cabinet meeting

chairman of the committee

Chancellor of the Exchequer

Conservative Party

Corporation Tax

Department of the Environment

First Lord of the Treasury

Foreign and Commonwealth Office

freedom of the press

Her Majesty

hon. and learned member

hon. gentleman
House of Commons
House of Lords
Houses of Parliament
in the House of Commons
in the House of Lords
Labour Party
Leader of the House
Leader of the Opposition
Leader of the Party
Liberal Party
Lord Privy Seal
Member of Parliament
my hon. and gallant friend
Metrication Board
Ministry of Defence
Ministry of Overseas Development

my hon. friend
National Insurance Act
Parliamentary Committee
Prime Minister
proportional representation
question time
rank and file
Retail Price Index
right honourable
right hon. gentleman
Secretary of State
Secretary of State for Scotland
Secretary of State for Wales
Solicitor General
social security
social security benefit
supplementary benefit

Legal

articles of association
as the case may be
ascertain the fact

assets and liabilities
at the date of
by reason of the fact

Chancery Division
Central Criminal Court
circumstantial evidence
counsel for the defence
counsel for the defendant
counsel for the plaintiff
counsel for the prisoner
counsel for the prosecution
Court of Appeal
Court of Appeal (Criminal Division)
deed of assignment
deed of settlement
deed of transfer
documentary evidence
documents of title
examination-in-chief
Family Division
grand jury
Habeas Corpus
heirs, executors, administrators and assigns
heirs, executors, administrators or assigns

High Court of Justice
judgment summons
justice of the peace
justices of the peace
King's Bench
King's Bench Division
King's Counsel
learned counsel
learned counsel for the defence
learned judge
legal estate
legal personal representative
Lord Chancellor
Lord Chief Justice
magistrates' court
marriage settlement
may it please your Honour
may it please your Lordship
memorandum of association
my learned friend
Official Receiver
originating summons

power of attorney 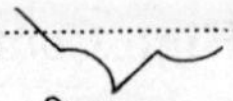

prima facie 

Queen's Bench 

Queen's Bench Division 

Queen's Counsel 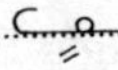

reversionary interest 

Supreme Court of Appeal 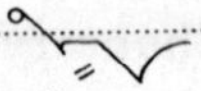

trust funds 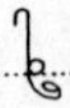

verdict for the defendant 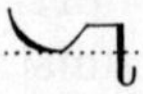

verdict for the plaintiff 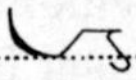

will and testament 

your Worship 

Longhand Keys to Reading and Writing Practice

Unit One

Passage 1

You were proposing to come in to the offices to[10] see us last week when the language conference was being[20] held. We were very sorry you found it impossible, as[30] your contribution would have been of value to us all.[40] Next week would be an even better time because we[50] have visitors working in our line of business coming in[60] from all over the world. So, if it is not[70] too inconvenient for you, we shall expect you on Monday[80] next, and we have arranged a programme especially for you[90] that will help you in your course. We shall expect[100] you unless we hear from you to the contrary by[110] telephone. Some of the best speakers in the world will[120] be with us here next week, and they will give[130] addresses on a wide range of subjects. For a different[140] reason, it will also be a good time to come[150] because our new conference hall is expected to be ready[160] for use, and that in itself will be worth the[170] experience. The decorators whose plans we adopted have done some[180] unusually fine work, and the hall is equipped with every[190] modern device in the matter of visual and audio aids[200] and is the last word in labour-saving easy-learning[210] techniques.

We shall spend the weekend after the conference in[220] analysing the results, because we have to make some very[230] vital decisions about our methods of carpet manufacture, and these[240] are a particular worry for us at this time as[250] the decisions will have to be taken almost immediately. Our[260] new workshops are all due to be built, and their[270] size and design will depend upon the choice of manufacturing[280] method that we make. I wish myself that I could[290] see ahead just for the next two or three years.[300] I will indicate why. It seems fairly certain that this[310] week the choice will come down to dense tufted carpets[320] of a plain colour or with pattern produced only by[330] texture or to tufted carpets with the full range of[340] bright colours and clearly defined patterns worked on the basis[350] of computer-fed colour threads. (**355** words)

Passage 2

From the beginning of the year, or even before that,[10] holiday-makers start making their plans to take holidays later[20] in the year. Many separate factors have to be given[30] consideration. There is the matter of ensuring that the accommodation[40] is good, the time of the year when the holiday[50] is to be taken will affect decisions, and the usual[60] arguments over the choice of locality will arise in which[70] the majority view has to prevail because, with many different[80] places to choose from, it is rare to find everybody[90] in agreement. Then there is the reality of cost, and[100] the possibility that this year the price may not be[110] right. If it is convenient for the whole family to[120] go away together, then the suitability of the type of[130] holiday and the place chosen will certainly enter into the[140] discussion. A location will have to be decided upon where[150] the majority can get the type of activity that they[160] like when on holiday. Many different travel companies offer holidays.[170] A wise thing will be to consult some authority on[180] the reliability of the firm chosen especially if this is[190] the first time. Even when you have it all worked[200] out to the best of your ability and you feel[210] that you have looked at all the possibilities from beginning[220] to end and have accomplished the task of squaring the[230] circle, there is still a chance that you may have[240] missed some vital point. (**244** words)

Unit Two

Passage 3

You will remember that in November of last year I[10] said that I thought our group was in for a[20] rough time. Whenever there is a setback in world trade,[30] we, as manufacturers of products that customers can do without,[40] are among the first to feel the pinch. When sales[50] fell, our financial resources were strained, and it was expensive[60] to keep on our complete labour force. Yet it would[70] have been a serious mistake to do otherwise. I believed[80] then, and I believe now, that workers, management and shareholders[90] have to stand together whatever hazards threaten, and there is[100] an advantage on balance to each of the parties in[110] doing so. Besides, whatever conditions may be in other areas,[120] our own relationships within the group with our staff and[130] work force have always remained first class.

By February or[140] March of this year, that is within four months, some[150] members of our trading group had been forced to go[160] on to part-time working, in the mistaken view that[170] they were unwise to accumulate stocks. We stayed confident that[180] we were capable of selling all our accumulated stocks, though[190] whether or not we could do so without loss remained[200] a question. Nevertheless, by the end of the trading year,[210] our books balanced and we came out marginally on the[220] right side. All our stocks, mostly of electrical appliances, have[230] been sold or are likely to be sold within a[240] month. We remembered the lessons of the past, and had[250] our new plans ready to go into action this spring.[260]

So well have our early sales gone that we have[270] every chance of doing very well over the year as[280] a whole, and it may well be that we shall[290] be back to 15 per cent profit by the end[300] of the period.

(**303** words)

Passage 4

The report that follows is made at the request of[10] the Court in order to assist them in their inquiries[20] about the Hawker family. Whatever advantages James Hawker had as[30] a boy, he very soon frittered away as a youth.[40] Most of the folk in that neighbourhood who can still[50] remember him believe that he was born evil, as it[60] seems some few are. Within a little time his thefts,[70] acts of violence and cruelty, and total disregard for the[80] welfare of any but himself brought him to the notice[90] of the law. Perhaps his only redeeming feature was his[100] generosity, and whenever he had money he would spend it[110] freely on himself and his cronies, buying them expensive gifts.[120] It was possibly this that influenced Rose Waring, an attractive[130] but wanton girl, to take some notice of him in[140] November 1938. They married after a[150] drunken spree and had five children in the period up[160] to 1949. Rose Waring was[170] not long in realizing the mistake she had made. James[180] Hawker continued his career of vicious crime and spent four[190] years in prison between 1938 and[200] 1949. (**205** words)

Unit Three

Passage 5

During the last decade we have grown rapidly and we[10] have taken a large suite of offices and opened a[20] library in premises at Swiss Cottage. However, we still keep[30] a small office in Central London. In this period a[40] number of our titles have become best-sellers in their[50] field. Three that have given us particular pleasure, and that[60] in the opinion of most people qualified to judge have[70] been the finest books on their subject ever published, have[80] been 'How we are Governed', 'Government and the People' and[90] 'A Description of Macro-Economics'.

Yet when things are going[100] swimmingly that is the time to get ready for fortune[110] to swing the other way. In the last year, we[120] have had a swarm of troubles to contend with. The[130] delivery of paper to our printing works has been halted[140] on more than one occasion by strikes and deficiencies. So[150] a number of books that should have been published have[160] been put off or cancelled. Several of our best people[170] on the editorial side have left us to start up[180] on their own, and we have not been able to[190] dissuade them from leaving us. The government has increased taxation[200] so that we can no longer afford to pay people[210] to represent us in Australasia, and we have two law-suits[220] pending through the Trade Descriptions Act. (**226** words)

Passage 6

Government involvement in matters that were once regarded as the[10] responsibility of the people themselves has been a fundamental feature[20] of life in modern societies all over the world during[30] the last few decades. Social change by government order has[40] been the method employed and, in the opinion of some,[50] the public has been governed as much by inter-departmental[60] decree and orders in council as by the legislation of[70] the House.

Yet it would be wrong to complain that[80] government has proceeded from the publication of papers and the[90] actions of the Civil Service. The fact is that whatever[100] has happened has been with majority public consent. Had there[110] been a powerful enough opposition, the politicians would have been[120] forced to change their line. Perhaps we are today a[130] more sentimental people than we were two centuries ago, readier[140] to have feelings about those in need and to take[150] action to care for them. Only we have decided that[160] our government is the repository of our charity and good[170] will, and must act on our part for the common[180] weal. Whatever the reasons, the facts are that local and[190] national government between them now play by far the major[200] role in education, health, welfare, social security, the protection of[210] our youth and of the mentally ill, and they exercise[220] a powerful veto against any action considered to be detrimental[230] to these concerns. And the list given is far from[240] being comprehensive. (**242** words)

Unit Four

Passage 7

It is only natural that one characteristic of children in[10] their early years should be that they are self-willed[20] and self-centred. The youth of every species has one[30] dominant instinct and that is to survive, and investigation by[40] Doctor Wolff, a specialist in biological research, shows that of[50] all animals, man is the one that demands maximum care[60] and maternal attention and has the minimum ability to survive[70] without years of help. Only after a decade or more[80] can the youth, whether boy or girl, become self-supporting.[90]

So unless children are to grow up aggressive and wholly[100] anti-social, self-seeking and without virtues, the training of[110] character and the general inculcation of social and moral values[120] must form a vital part of their early lives. In[130] the circumstances of today, it is questionable whether there is[140] sufficient of such training either in the school or in[150] the home. In centuries past, opinion was unanimous that such[160] moral and social training, largely through religious teaching, had an[170] essential role in the making of men and women. We[180] have exchanged too much severity in these matters for too[190] much freedom. Unless the stage of self-discipline and correct[200] social attitudes has been reached, too much freedom leads to[210] licence, and that in its turn to anarchy, and to[220] the possible victory of the strong and the wicked over[230] the weak and the good. (**235** words)

Passage 8

A large business such as ours always aims to carry[10] on with the minimum amount of involvement in politics, and[20] above all must be seen not to favour one party[30] at the expense of another. Yet it is questionable whether,[40] in the sort of world in which we live, and[50] also, because of the general legislation on economic matters that[60] is a feature of modern government policies, we can ever[70] succeed. Circumstances were different a century ago. Then the policy[80] of the ruling party was to let business and workers[90] get on without interference. But looking backwards to that period[100] of history, we find many of its characteristics obnoxious to[110] us today whatever party we ourselves vote for.

Henceforward, we[120] believe that we must look forward, not backward, and play[130] the maximum part we are allowed to play in shaping[140] government policy to help and foster trade and commerce as[150] best we may. This means that we also have a[160] duty to look outward and not inward, to consult our[170] own workers and business rivals as well as what is[180] good for the whole nation. In such an exchange of[190] views among representatives of all sections of opinion in the[200] country lies the best hope for the future. The general[210] well-being of the people will bring us its own[220] reward in higher sales and profits especially in a business[230] like ours so sensitive to personal spending power. It would[240] be too much to expect that we are ever likely[250] to reach policies unanimously agreed, but we should certainly support[260] any straightforward issue in which the general good is manifest,[270] though the decisions to be taken may be not wholly[280] to the liking of every small party or every wayward[290] section of opinion. This is why we are ready to[300] place advertisements in the newspapers expressing our views in a[310] rational way. This is why we ask for your support for the introduction of the financial measures now proposed. (**329** words)

Unit Five

Passage 9

It is interesting to notice that the interest charges on the loans we have raised in order to set up Great Britain Properties Limited are the lowest for many years, and I am sure that you will agree with me that this is a matter for self-congratulation, in particular for Mr. Robert Lowe, our chief bank executive.

I would call your special attention to the fact that our contract excludes any extra charges except in so far as special charges may be necessary because of the peculiar requirements of our clients in the organization of their productive activities in the southern region of Great Britain. The regular requirements of the financial interests involved in these deals, all conducted within the regular forms needed by the legislature provisions of the contract, have been correctly provided for. We have the full support of our merchant bank. The Bank of England has given its blessing to our plans. On the other side of the coin we have to accept large telephone bills for the many overseas calls that have had to be made, and the electricity bills that will be incurred as a result of the large-scale excavations needed in the early stages of building will, we are sure, be high.

We must be sure that regular attention is given to the needs of the work force and that, as far as we can make it, all supplies and services for the contract are self-contained. (**245** words)

Passage 10

The factors that affect production are many and various. Very often, too, they are peculiar and not easily to be predicted. For this reason, those with a special interest in manufacturing production have, on more than one occasion, pointed out that the successful management of an organization, the prime function of which is to produce goods, is almost sure to be sometimes as much a matter of luck or chance and intuitive guessing as it is of executive know-how or of regular management skills that may be acquired by study and practice. As a generalization, it could be said that the lucky manager is one who is inspired to make more correct choices than wrong ones.

If we think[120] about production in a steady market when, as a hypothesis,[130] the total volume of manufactures sold remains regular and constant,[140] we now ask: 'What are the factors that affect production?'[150] We shall come nowhere near an exhaustive list, but at[160] least we may be sure of some certain elements that[170] will change production in one way or another. First, of[180] course, is the effectiveness of the work force. Have they[190] a true interest in the total production of the organization?[200] Is it worthwhile for them to work better and harder?[210] Do they show signs of cheerfulness and are they fully[220] aware of the usefulness of their jobs? Are there restrictive[230] practices that have to be contended with? Then there is[240] the question of the executives who organize supplies and materials[250] and the problems and difficulties that they may face. A[260] sudden shortage of a single component may affect production just[270] as surely as though the work force were to go[280] on strike. Legislation by the government may just as surely[290] act as a brake on production or as a spur.[300] It is a peculiar fact of our times that most[310] legislative action seems to hinder production more than it helps[320] it. (**321** words)

Unit Six

Passage 11

Great Britain has been in serious economic difficulties almost ever[10] since the Second World War and the situation has grown[20] worse in the last few years. A principal result has[30] been the fall off in the number of jobs. The[40] performance of our industrial firms over the past few years[50] offers no justification for much hope for the future. Yet[60] the fault lies only in small part on management which[70] very often produces a whole new class of young business[80] executives, all intelligent individuals, and keen to get business moving[90] again. Jobs have become fewer because, owing to high taxation[100] and government intervention in business affairs, and because of high[110] labour costs, too, profits have been low and in the[120] last two or three years non-existent. Too many people[130] are self-centred and self-seeking. Industry cannot make any[140] upward progress unless it is entirely self-supporting. When profits[150] are in danger, management will not make investment of capital[160] for new plant.

A recent investigation has shown that in[170] the last five years there have been twice as many[180] business failures as in the previous five years. (**188** words)

Passage 12

Captain Black was born the child of a poor farm[10] labourer in the northern part of Cumbria in 1909.[20] As a boy he had no advantages, yet[30] by self-discipline and a cheerfulness of spirit that has[40] always been a chief characteristic, he rose to great success.[50] When he was only 14 years old, his uncle got[60] him a place as cabin boy on a ship making[70] regular runs to South America. John Black had a passion[80] for study and a great love of the sea. His[90] carefulness over small matters and his fearlessness in all situations[100] made their mark. He worked hard and in the fullness[110] of time he passed his examinations for his Master's Certificate[120] as a ship's captain. However, this was at the time[130] of the great depression and no ships were available. So[140] with his savings he bought a small brickyard and in[150] the space of a few years he had organized it[160] so that its production of bricks was doubled and he[170] employed four representatives selling his high quality hard bricks all[180] over the country.

It was inevitable that when the war[190] came he should join the Navy. He rose through his[200] skill and prowess to be the captain of a capital[210] ship, the aircraft carrier 'Royal Swan'. He served with distinction[220] for the most part in northern waters. Afterwards he bought[230] a vineyard in France, as he had always been a[240] lover of France and after a period when he came[250] near to losing everything, he raised the capital necessary to[260] improve the vineyard and in a limited period of five[270] years he paid off the interest charges and the whole[280] of the borrowed capital. (**284** words)

Unit Seven

Passage 13

The National Health scheme which began in the United Kingdom[10] in 1948 was certainly a remarkable[20] social measure. It was greeted with public enthusiasm, and 5[30] July is a day to be inscribed on our calendars.[40] The instructions to the Secretary of State for Social Services[50] were to set up a full national health service to[60] improve the physical and mental health of the people, to[70] prevent illness and to treat it whenever it arose. It[80] is no surprise that the people of Great Britain gave[90] it an enthusiastic welcome.

Today the National Health Service has[100] run into rough water, and indeed some people have remarked[110] that its very existence has been endangered. The truth is[120] that the nation would not accept its abandonment. The government[130] department discharged its duties well and for twenty years the[140] scheme ran satisfactorily till it became defective, particularly during the[150] past ten years. Independent research bodies have remarked on the[160] main reasons for its weaknesses in recent years, and it[170] is instructive to note what these main reasons are. First[180] there has been the great rise in costs as the[190] work of the Service has expanded. This is familiar enough[200] to us all but it has been made worse by[210] the constant rise in administration both in numbers and in[220] cost, more especially as a result of the local government[230] re-organization of a few years back which many now see[240] as a thoroughly bad measure, though it is true they[250] may be looking at it in a too subjective way.[260] Too much is spent on too many bureaucrats and too[270] little on the actual Service. (**275** words)

Passage 14

I am sure you will be glad to know that[10] Mr. Jack Fields, our enthusiastic young executive, whose ability you[20] remarked upon when you were making your familiarization tour of[30] all our branches, has agreed to act as editor of[40] the Production Conference Report this year. If you have any[50] special instructions for him would you please let me have[60] them before the end of the month. Jack Fields will[70] discharge this task with truth and fearlessness. He will cross-[80] examine all those who have put forward claims that seem[90] to us to lack justification, and he will continue with[100] a relentlessness surprising in such a young man till the[110] truth is revealed. Further, he is an unselfish man not[120] in the least inconsiderate of the rights and feelings of[130] others.

What I am remarking on really is that you[140] need not have fears that he will endanger our business[150] relationships because of his enthusiasm or his independence of mind.[160] I have as much faith in his subjective judgments as[170] I have in his down-to-earth familiarity with the[180] whole of our area of operations. (**186** words)

Unit Eight

Passage 15

In an inflationary period of history such as the one[10] the world has been coping with for the past thirty[20] years, the people who tend to take pessimistic views and[30] who consider everything that happens objectively are those most likely[40] to escape its worst effects. A strong nerve is indispensable[50] in times when prices are rising each month and the[60] value of money is falling. In using resources both of[70] money and of ability to the best advantage, you have[80] to be able to distinguish between what may appear on[90] the surface to be similar situations, yet in fact are[100] far from identical, and which need objective and conservative thinking[110] in order to distinguish the success from the failure. Too[120] optimistic a view may lead to a heavy financial loss;[130] too pessimistic an attitude may result in a missed opportunity[140] and for similar reasons. Each of us, if we are[150] to ride the inflationary wave with any success, must do[160] all that is practicable to deal with each contingency as[170] it arises. If the price of electricity soars then we[180] must change immediately to oil heaters. If the country is[190] a poor performer in the foreign exchange market, then we[200] must take our holidays locally instead of abroad. (**208** words)

Passage 16

Over one hundred fellow members of the Institute and I[10] set out last Friday for a tour of the Louis[20] XV Vineyard, and on this occasion the gods were[30] kind to us and blessed us with warm and sunny[40] weather. The expected arrangements were that we would go first[50] on an inspection of the lovely mansion that is adjacent[60] to the vineyard, and then go on a tour of[70] the very fine formal gardens that were laid out early[80] in the seventeenth century. On this occasion we had, in[90] M. Jacques, a first-class guide speaking good, clear English.[100] His knowledge was remarkable and he was always ready to[110] give further information if asked. In the house which was[120] at one time the established home of Louis himself, he[130] concentrated on the art objects and the pictures of which[140] there are a great number now in the charge of[150] the Ministry of Fine Arts. The noblemen who still own[160] the house handed authority over to the Ministry for the[170] care and upkeep of all art objects and pictures about[180] four years ago. On this section of the tour he[190] showed us the magnificent rubies that have been the heirlooms[200] of this distinguished family for more than five centuries since[210] they moved out of Brittany into this part of France. (**220** words)

Unit Nine

Passage 17

The destructive instincts of man are well known. In some[10] respects we give them a safety valve through games such[20] as coconut shies and plate smashing at fair grounds or[30] in striking balls savagely over nets or down fairways. But[40] the destruction of the property of ratepayers or of citizens[50] in general is a feature of our restless, rootless metropolitan[60] life and it has become a substantial problem for the[70] police and for the local authorities.

On the face of[80] it, severe punishment would seem to be the answer for[90] any persons caught, but it is doubtful whether it is[100] really effective. Judicial punishment or school punishment respectively do not[110] seem to do any good. Reformers are right when they[120] point out that if reform is to be carried out,[130] then it should be reform directed at the root causes[140] of the destructive urge. Although the difficulties of dealing with[150] these root causes are great, a growing number of our[160] fellow citizens subscribe to the idea that we should aim[170] at a cure rather than merely to deter possible offenders.[180] The cost to the ratepayers of the destruction of public[190] property that goes on, especially in large metropolitan areas, is[200] really frightening and it seems to rise every year. Call[210] boxes, bus stops and every sort of telegraphic equipment, empty[220] houses and public notices all seem to be particularly the[230] target of the vandal. If you live in a town,[240] you can be no stranger to the evidence of destruction.[250] More than the government or the local authorities think, people[260] hold the view that we have lost our way. Respect[270] for what belongs to individuals or to us all, the[280] idea of right and wrong and the fact that everyone[290] should be able to rely on his neighbour being trustworthy,[300] are values that neither the family nor the school seem[310] to inculcate in these days. So many people show no[320] sensibility or social sense. They do not see that the[330] stranger just as much as one's own family has the[340] same rights and that we each have responsibilities for one[350] another. (**351** words)

Passage 18

I have been instructed to speak to you all today[10] with reference to the reforms recently introduced dealing with cargoes[20] for shipment at home and overseas. Most probably, you will[30] know something of this already, and to a great extent[40] this talk may be a repetition of the facts of[50] the case with which you are already familiar. However, it[60] will not be out of place to have it on[70] record. On 14 June, by Acts of Parliament passed in[80] the House of Commons on that day, some changes in[90] the laws for the loading and security of some shipments[100] which you make from time to time will come into[110] force on 1 November. You may also know that some[120] differences of opinion arose in the debates, and we have[130] now heard from the Ministry that, in point of fact,[140] some amending legislation is likely before that day.

The Ministry[150] has been under extreme pressure from shipping firms like ourselves[160] to make exceptions in respect to certain shipments, a list[170] of which is available. We have no objection to some[180] clauses of the Acts, but we have put up a[190] list of questions on doubtful points for which we have[200] asked to have yes or no replies. As the date[210] of enforcement comes nearer and nearer we shall put on[220] as much pressure as we can to get these points[230] clarified.

We expect to receive answers, and as soon as[240] they arrive we will inform you of them. We hope[250] you will agree with what we have been doing, and as[260] our attitudes towards one another have always been sensible and[270] correct, we know we can rely on you to let[280] us know of any difference of opinion you may have.[290] We need to get together in order to set up[300] national representation in these matters. (**305** words)

Unit Ten

Passage 19

Membership application for admission to the Historical Society is to[10] be made on the enclosed application form. We have recently[20] amalgamated with the Archaeological Society, and one result of the[30] amalgamation is that we seek to increase the proportion of[40] our members who have a knowledge of archaeology and some[50] interests in the field, especially that of the architectural styles[60] of the Far East during the Christian era. This is[70] a neglected area of study in which you will no[80] doubt be able to make a significant contribution to the[90] proceedings of our Society. The splendid Japanese items that you[100] sent us have been passed on to the administrator of[110] our museum. Please visit the museum even though your application[120] is not yet through. Formal application is necessary even for[130] the best qualified like yourself. Among many wonderful items you[140] will find some rather monstrous ones, but it is our[150] misfortune that we have no funds for a full-time[160] curator and the display of items is arbitrary and out[170] of all proportion to their relative importance.

We cannot blame[180] our administrator who works in his leisure and receives no[190] fees. However, a court case still under arbitration may very[200] well bring us, as a gift from the executors of[210] the late Sir Walter Wood, a new building to house[220] our collection. If this happens, the university have said that[230] they will pay a large proportion of the salary of[240] a qualified curator and administrator. In view of the universality[250] of your interests in history and archaeology, is this a[260] post that your present leisure would enable you to take[270] on?

I look forward to meeting you at the new[280] Projects Committee when you will be introduced to leading members[290] of the Society Council. (**294** words)

Passage 20

Ladies and Gentlemen, We are assembled here to hold an[10] extraordinary general meeting, the purpose of which is to decide[20] upon the proposed amalgamation of the country and metropolitan divisions[30] of the company. You are, I hope, already in possession[40] of the Report. It will be my duty to act[50] as chairman and I am a substitute for Sir John[60] who has a chill and cannot be with us. He[70] is very sorry for his absence today. You have already[80] heard that Jane South and Tom Gowers are here. He[90] will explain the reasons for the change and she will[100] follow with an account of the financial arrangements. They will[110] between them answer any questions you have on the Report.[120] I will do my best to secure a fair hearing[130] for everyone.

Tom Gowers is head of our Policy Committee[140] and he is well known to most of you. Jane[150] South, our brilliant accountant, came to us a year ago[160] from National Motors and she is, off the record, this[170] year's Senior Accounting Prize Winner. Perhaps that is enough in[180] the way of introduction. We are not here for any[190] other purpose and members have not the right at this[200] meeting to raise any other issue. It is not allowed[210] under Standing Orders for such meetings. I am sure you[220] will all understand and accept this.

The Board would not[230] have called such a meeting were not they anxious to[240] find out your views on the amalgamation and it would[250] not be correct for me to accept any comment that[260] I am sure is irrelevant. May I also inform you[270] that the meeting should not—indeed, it cannot—extend beyond[280] 5 p.m. I will, therefore, limit each speaker from[290] the floor to two minutes. Now we're ready and you're[300] welcome to smoke if you wish. (**306** words)

Unit Eleven

Passage 21

Royal occasions often require railway travel. On such occasions British[10] Rail make available a special royal train which is used[20] only by senior members of the Royal Family. The royal[30] train provides all the facilities of a first-class hotel[40] and so enables members of the Royal Family to move[50] from one engagement to another with the minimum of fatigue[60] and trouble. It is usual for a royal car to[70] bring the royal party to the railway station from which[80] they will set out on their journey. The timetables of[90] local railways are adjusted to allow free passage for the[100] royal train with the minimum of obstruction to normal services.[110] Planning such a journey is a mathematical exercise in which[120] the executives of the British Railways Board are especially skilled.[130] Of course, when the whole family travels, room is made[140] for the royal nurse and preparations are made for a[150] royal welcome by the loyal citizens of the place to[160] be visited.

A number of local authorities in all parts[170] of the United Kingdom still retain the title of Royal[180] Borough and these all date from the past, often centuries[190] ago, when some towns were granted Royal Charters, sometimes for[200] single acts of loyalty to the crown, sometimes for large[210] monetary gifts. (**212** words)

Passage 22

Colonel Jackson, writing in the Financial Journal, points out that[10] in his school days, he was taught the relationships between[20] fractions and percentages, and states how valuable this knowledge has[30] been to him all his life. For example, 12½[40] per cent is an eighth, 37½[50] per cent is three-eighths, 2½[60] per cent is one-fortieth, and 1¼[70] per cent is one-eightieth. These are worth remembering[80] along with the usual ones like 25 per cent[90] being one-quarter and 75 per cent being three-[100]quarters and so on. Such knowledge is particularly useful when,[110] as in our business, we have to carry out many[120] operations in which French francs, Swiss francs and Deutschmarks are[130] to be converted into sterling or vice versa.

When rates[140] of exchange are changing daily, tables are of no use[150] and all these sums have to be done on a[160] day-to-day basis. It is quite common, for example,[170] to have to work out what, say, £42,000[180] is in lire and then to work out from[190] that what the total will be if the lire are[200] to be paid in Deutschmarks. Our Exchange Superintendent has a[210] short training course for new entrants to his department in[220] which dealing with Swiss francs or Australian dollars is a[230] vital part of the work, especially as we keep a[240] number of accounts in Swiss banks.

Before new entrants go[250] on to the staff, he has to have the assurance[260] of his own practical experience with these people that they[270] have the right mastery of arithmetic to be able to[280] change £34,000 into lire and then at[290] the current rates state what payment will be needed from[300] lire into American dollars or French francs. Every day will[310] produce a slightly different result. Half our success depends, as[320] we said in the Foreign Exchange Journal, on intelligent forecasts[330] of what the rates may be in a week or[340] a month.

(**342** words)

Alphabetical list of short forms and some derivatives

a		arbitrary	
accord/according to		arbitrate	
accordingly		arbitration	
acknowledge		arbitrator	
administrator		architect/architectural/ architecture	
advantage		are	
advertise/ advertisement		as	
all		balance	
almost		be	
also		because	
although		before	
altogether		behalf	
always		belief/believe	
amalgamate		beyond	
amalgamation		build/building	
an		but	
and		cannot	
any		capable	
anybody		certificate	
anyhow		character	
anyone		characteristic	
anything		child	

circumstance

circumstances

circumstantial

cold

commercial/ commercially

contingency

could

cross-examination/ cross-examine

danger

dangerously

dear

defective

deficient/deficiently/ deficiency

deliver/delivery

deliverance

demonstrate

demonstration

demonstrator

description

destruction

destructive

destructively

develop

development

difference/different

difficult

difficulty

discharge

disrespect

disrespectful

distinguish

do

doctor, Dr.

dollar

during

efficient/efficiency/ efficiently

emergency

endanger

enlarge

enlargement

enlarger

enthusiasm/ enthusiastic

especial/especially

establish/ establishment

everything

exchange

executive

executor

exigency
expect
expediency
expenditure
expensive
extinguish
eye
familiar/familiarity
familiarization
familiarize
February
financial/financially
first
for
from
general/generally
generalization
gentleman
gentlemen
govern
government
great
had
hand

handle
handler
has
have
himself
his
hour
how
however
howsoever
I
identical
identification
immediate
imperfect/imperfection/imperfectly
imperturbable
important/importance
impossible
in
inconsiderate
inconvenience/inconvenient/inconveniently
incorporate
independence/independent/independently

indispensable/ indispensably

individual/ individually

inflationary

influence

influential

inform

information

informer

inscribe

inscription

inspect/inspection

institute

institution

instruction

instructive

insurance

intelligence

intelligent/ intelligently

intelligible/ intelligibly

interest

introduction

investigation

investment

irrecoverable/ irrecoverably

irregular

irremovable/ irremovably

irrespective

irrespectively

irresponsible/ irresponsibility

is

it

its

itself

January

jurisdiction

justification

knowledge

knowledgeable

language

large

largely

larger

largest

legislative

legislature

liberty

listless

manufacture

manufacturer	neglect
manuscript	negligence
mathematical/ mathematically	nevertheless
mathematician	next
mathematics	nor
maximum	northern
mechanical/ mechanically	nothing
member	notwithstanding
mere	November
messenger	number
metropolitan	O
minimum	object
ministry	objection
misfortune	objectionable
mistake	objective
mistaken	objectively
monstrous	obstruction
more	obstructive
Mr.	obstructively
Mrs.	of
mortgage	oh
mostly	on
myself	oneself
near	opinion

opportunity	postal
optimistic	postcard
organization	postcode
organize	postfree
organizer	postman
ought	postmaster
our	postpone
ourselves	postscript
owe	practicable
parliament	practice/practise
parliamentary	prejudice/prejudicial/ prejudicially
particular	preliminary
particularly	principal/principally/ principle
passenger	probable/probably/ probability
peculiar/peculiarity	production
people	productive
perform	productivity
performance	project
performer	proportion
perpendicular	proportionate/ proportionately
perspective	prospect
pessimistic	prospective
pleasure	prospectus
postage	public/publicly/ publish

- publication
- publisher
- put
- questionable/ questionably
- ratepayers
- rather
- recoverable
- reform
- reformer
- regular
- remark
- remarkable/ remarkably
- remember
- remonstrance
- remonstrate
- removable
- represent
- representation
- representative
- republic
- republican
- respect
- respective
- respectively

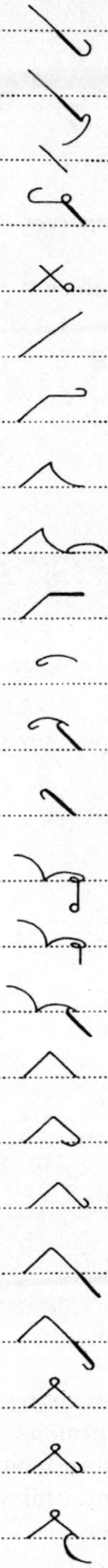

- responsible/ responsibility
- restless
- retrospect
- restrospection
- retrospective
- retrospectively
- satisfaction
- satisfactory
- selfish/selfishness
- sensible/sensibly/ sensibility
- several
- shall
- short
- shorthand
- should
- significance
- significant/signify
- signification
- something
- southern
- speak
- special/specially
- stranger
- stringency

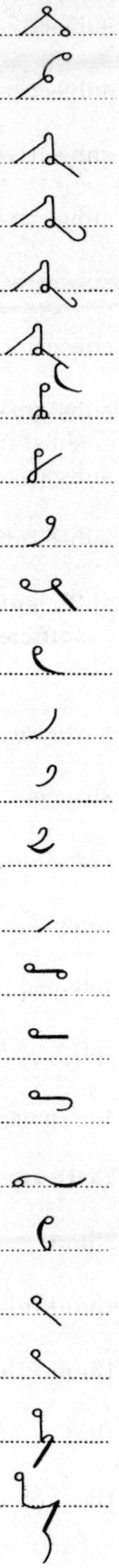

subject
subjection
subjective
subjectively
subscribe
subscription
substantial/substantially
substitute
substitution
sufficient/sufficiently/sufficiency
sure
surprise
suspect
tasteful
telegram
telegraphic
tell
testimony
textbook
thank
thankful
thankfulness
that
the

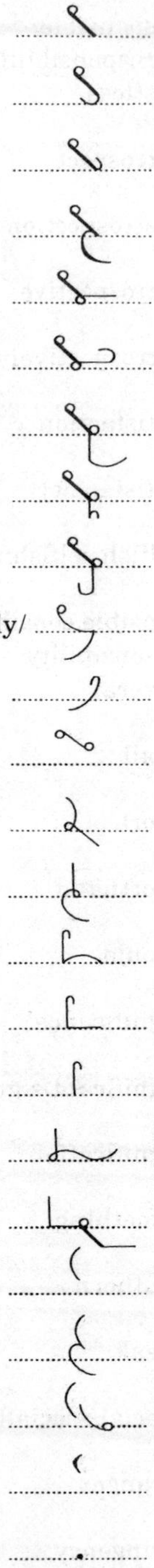

there
their
them
themselves
therefore
thing
think
this
till
to
too
today
tomorrow
to be
together
told
two
toward
trade
trade-in
truth
trustworthy
unanimous/unanimously/unanimity
under

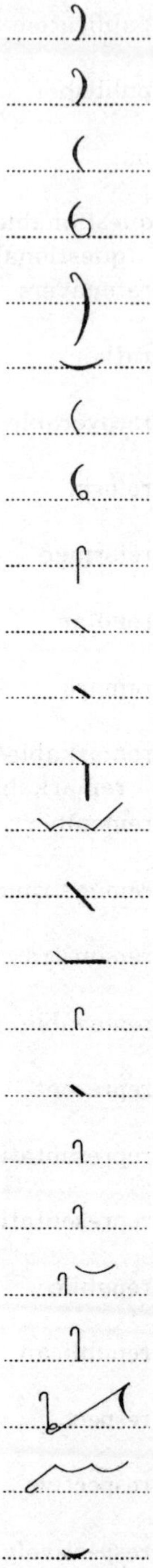

understand
understood
unfortunately
uniform/uniformity/ uniformly
universal/universally
universality
universe
university
unprincipled
usual/usually
valuation
very
wasteful
we
what
whatever
whatsoever
when
whenever
whensoever
wheresoever
whether

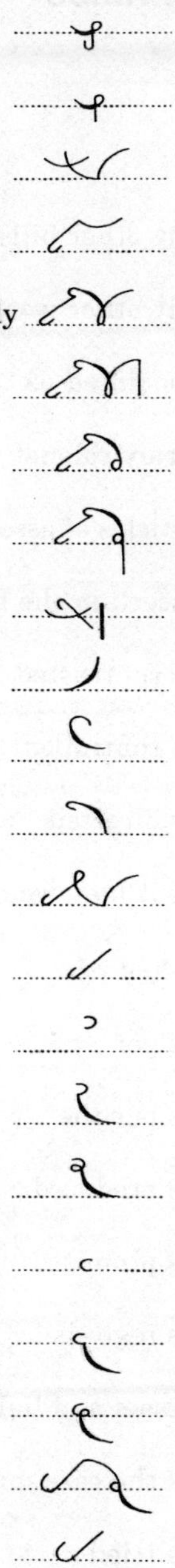

which
who
whose
why
will
wish
with
within
without
wonderful/ wonderfully
worthwhile
would
writer
year
yesterday
you
your
yourself
yourselves
young
younger
youngster

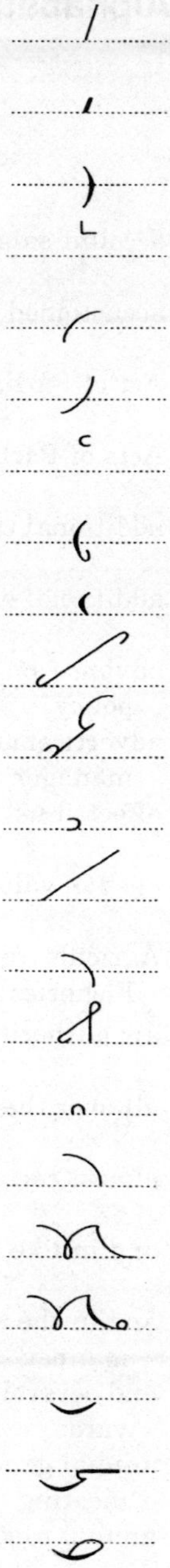

Alphabetical list of useful phrases

account sales	any other bills
accustomed policy	any other words
Act of Parliament	appointed us
Acts of Parliament	Army colonel
additional cost	articles of association
additional expense	ascertain the fact
advance against a life policy	as contrasted
advertisement manager	as controlled
affected us	as directed
agent's valuation	as it may well
Agriculture, Fisheries and Food	asked us
air authorities	as per
all over the world	as per the
almost certain	as produced
and in like manner	as promised
and in the same manner	as regards
and several thousand yards	assets and liabilities
annual general meeting	as the case may be
annual report	as tried
anticipated requirements	as we are
any information	as we can

as we cannot

as we can see

as we do

as we do not think

as we do not think there is

as we explained

as we feel

as we felt

as we had

as we had not

as we have

as we have been there

as we have not

as we have not been

as we know

as we know there is

as we invited

as we know we shall

as well

as well as

as well as can be

as well as it can

as well as last time

as well as possible

as well as usual

as we did not think there was

as we may

as we may be

as we produce

as we promised

as we see

as we shall

as we shall see

as we think

as we think there is

as we think we can

as we think we may

as we thought

as we tried

as we trust

as we want

as we went

as we wish

at any rate

at home

at home and abroad

at home and overseas

attacked us

at the beginning
at the date of
at the first reading
at the second reading
at the third reading
at work
at your convenience
at your earliest convenience
autumn morning
balance sheet
bank clerk
bank giro
bank manager
bank note
Bank of England
based on
base rate
bearer cheque
best of my ability
best of our ability
best of their ability
better governments
bill of lading
bills of lading

birth mark
Bishop of London
blessed us
blood pressure
board of directors
booked us
British association
British custom
British customs
British government
British Isles
British manufacture
British manufacturers
British Museum
British people
British production
British Rail
British railways
building charges
building society
by government
by order of the government
by reason of the fact
by return post

by return of post
cabinet meeting
called on
cancel the cheque
capable of
capital expenditure
capital gains
capital invested
capital investment
capital letters
capital punishment
capital ship
Captain Black
Captain Brown
car insurance
car parks
carried off the
carried on
carried out
carry on
cash dispenser
Central Criminal Court
Central Park
certain shipments

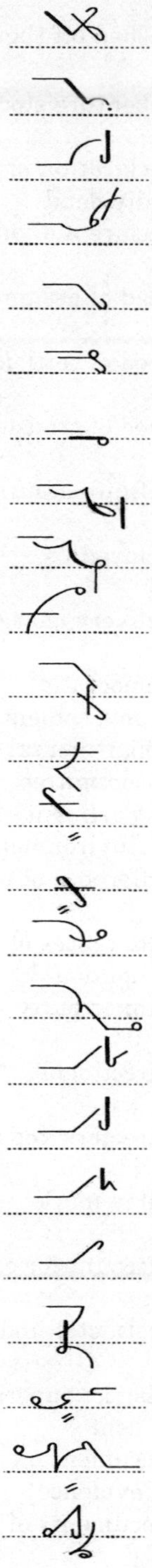

certificate of insurance
certified cheque
chairman of the committee
chairman said
Chancellor of the Exchequer
Chancery Appeal
Chancery division
Chancery Judge
Chancery Judges
Chancery Lane
Chancery records
cheque card
circumstantial evidence
City Park
civil authorities
clearing house
cocktail party
cold morning
College Professor
Colonel Jackson
Colonel Johnson
common words
company policy
comprehensive insurance

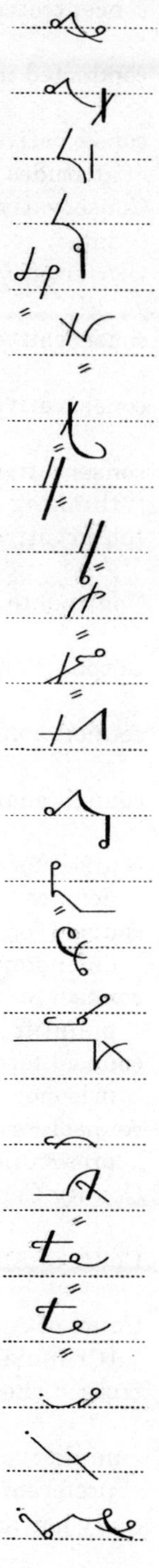

concentrated on	dashed off the
conducted us	debenture stock
conservative attitudes	declaration of a dividend
Conservative candidate	declare a dividend
Conservative Party	deed of assignment
conservative policy	deed of settlement
conservative scholars	deed of transfer
conservative thinking	definite assurance
conservative times	delayed us
Continental railways	delivery charges
Corporation Tax	democratic government
council approval	departmental committee
council chamber	Department of the Environment
counsel for the defence	difference of opinion
counsel for the defendant	differences of opinion
counsel for the plaintiff	dinner party
counsel for the prisoner	direct debit
counsel for the prosecution	directors' report
County Council	dirty mark
Court of Appeal	discount for cash
Court of Appeal (Criminal Division)	distinctly understood
crossed cheque	district superintendent
cumulative preference shares	documentary evidence
daily journal	documents of title

domestic insurance
do you mean to say
during the
during the last few weeks
during the last few years
during the next month
during the year
earlier on
earliest convenience
early morning
Economics Society
elected government
electricity bills
emergency requirements
endowment policy
established society
examination-in-chief
exchange superintendent
Executor and Trustee Department
expected arrangements
expected business
expected capital
expected charge
expected insurance

expected requirements
expected us
expect to receive
expenditure required
expression of opinion
extraordinary general meeting
extremely regret
extremely regrettable
extremely sorry
extreme pressure
fact of the matter
facts of the matter
facts of the case
fair valuation
Family Division
farmed out
farther on
fellow citizens
fellow directors
fellow members
fellow students
fellow tradesmen
fellow travellers
few words

financial department
fire insurance
First Lord of the Treasury
five or six
Foreign and Commonwealth Office
foreign national
for his information
formal application
formed society
form of application
for shipment
for their information
for their society
for the record
for the sake of
for your information
freedom of the press
Friday evening
Friday evenings
Friday next
from beginning to end
from the beginning
from the embankment
from their policies

furniture valuations
further information
further on
games captain
general inquiry
general insurance
giro credit
government deficiency
government official
government policies
government policy
government requirements
grand jury
grass bank
Great Britain
great embankments
greater part of
greater than
great number
great number of the
great part
great part of the
great part of the world
Green Park

Habeas Corpus
handed authority
handed us
hated us
have my assurance
he can say
he can see
heeded the convenience
he has received
heirs, executors, administrators and assigns
heirs, executors, administrators or assigns
he is not logical
Her Majesty
he will be instructed
he will have to say that
he would like to say a few words
High Court of Justice
higher authority
high pressure
high valuation
hire purchase agreement
hold forth
Home Secretary

hon. and learned member
hon. gentleman
house journal
House of Commons
House of Lords
Houses of Parliament
house to house
house valuation
how many words
hurried off
hurried out
Hyde Park
I am glad to move the adoption
I am in receipt of your letter
I am instructed
I am sorry to say
I am sure
I assure you
I believe
I carried out
if it is convenient
if it is not convenient
if it were
if it were not

- if we are logical
- if you carried on
- if you carried out
- if you were
- if you were not
- if you will instruct
- if your information
- I gave
- I give
- I have no objection
- I have pleasure
- I have received
- I have to say that
- important arrangements
- in a few words
- in a great measure
- in a word
- incorrect valuation
- individual requirements
- industrial relations
- in exchange
- inexpensive department
- inflationary pressures
- informed us

- inform me
- inform us
- in his opinion
- in his own words
- injured party
- in many words
- in moving the adoption of the report and accounts
- in my opinion
- in November
- in other respects
- in other words
- in our opinion
- in point of fact
- in reality
- in reference to
- in reference to which
- in regard to
- in reply to your letter
- in respect to
- insisted on the
- in some respects
- in some sections
- inspected forms
- instructed us

in such a manner as
insurance company
insurance depends
insurance policies
insurance policy
insurance premium
intelligence required
interest charge
interested authorities
interest required
interim dividend
intervened on
in the beginning
in the circumstances
in the first instance
in the hands of
in the house
in the House of Commons
in the House of Lords
in the last place
in the next place
in their opinion
in these sections
in these words

in the third place
in the world
in this house
in this section
in this world
in those words
into effect
investment management service
in which section
in which the party
in world trade
in yards
in your reply to my letter
I put forth
I remember
I remembered
I see no objection
is it convenient
I take no objection
it is agreed
it is also
it is assured
it is interesting
it is most interesting

it is my pleasure
it is my policy
it is not convenient
it is not logical
it is worth
it is worthless
it is worthy
it may also
it may also be
it may well be
I told
it will also be
it would be logical
I was beginning
I would like to say a few words
joint stock bank
journal entries
journal of medicine
judgment summons
judicial punishment
justice of the peace
King's Bench
King's Bench division
King's Counsel

Labour Party
lady superintendent
laid out
large number of
large number of inquiries
large numbers
last evening
last few weeks
last government
last indorser
last week
later on
law council
Leader of the House
Leader of the Opposition
Leader of the Party
learned counsel
learned counsel for the defence
learned judge
left hand
legal estate
legal personal representative
let us be sure
liberal measures

Liberal Party or
liberal portions
life insurance
life policies
limited availability
limited company
limited edition
limited knowledge
limited knowledge of the
limited number
limited payments
limited period
limited rewards
Lloyd Park
local authority
local bishop
local councils
local government
local parks
local railways
located us
Lord Chancellor
Lord Chief Justice
Lord Privy Seal

loved us
low pressure
low valuation
magistrates' court
major development
major disaster
major operation
major road
make application
male superintendent
managing director
man and woman
many words
many yards
marine insurance
marriage settlement
maximum ability
maximum charge
may it please your Honour
may it please your Lordship
member of
Member of Parliament
member of the
membership application

Members of Parliament

memorandum of association

men and women

merchant bank

messenger requires

Metrication Board

miniature railway

minimum ability

minimum charge

minimum requirements

Ministry of Defence

Ministry of Overseas Development

modern society

Monday evening

Monday evenings

Monday morning

Monday next

monthly report

more ability

morning session

most interested

most interesting

mostly require

most probably

motor-car insurance

moved out

Mr. and Mrs.

musical instrument

Music Professor

must be sure

my ability

my application

my assurance

my hon. and gallant friend

my hon. friend

my learned friend

my words

national authorities

national average

national economy

national expenditure

national future

national government

National Health

national insurance

National Insurance Act

national interest

national representation

national stage
national survey
nearer and nearer
necessary authority
needless to say
negotiable instrument
negotiable security
neither more nor less
neither this nor that
new capital
new policy
new ship
next door
next few weeks
next few years
next month
next week
no reality
north and south
not negotiable cheque
notwithstanding the fact
number of
number of companies
of buildings

office manager
Official Receiver
off the record
of the board
of the house
of the world
of this house
one another
one morning
one or two
only limited
on my authority
on such occasions
on the other
on the other hand
on these sections
on this occasion
on this section
or two
ordinary assurance
ordinary dividend
ordinary shareholders
originating summons
other governments

ought to have
ought to have known
our ability
our application
our assurance
our government
our valuation
out of place
out of the question
over and above
paid up capital
paid up capital of the company
Parliamentary Committee
party games
party organizer
passenger charges
passengers require
pasted on
past few weeks
paying-in slip
peculiar circumstances of the case
peculiar requirements
people require
people's attention

people's inquiries
per capita
per head
per minute
per month
please inform us
police superintendent
postal order
postpone arrangements
power of attorney
preference dividend
preference shareholders
preference shares
preliminary arrangements
preliminary inquiries
present no objection
prima facie
Prime Minister
principal charges
private secretary
probate valuation
production charges
professional journal
Professor of Chemistry

Professor of Economics
Professor of Music
Professor Thomas
profit and loss account
profit margin
proportional representation
provided convenient
public inquiry
public's requirements
publisher requires
put forth
Queen's Bench
Queen's Bench Division
Queen's Counsel
question time
quicker and quicker
railway line
railway station
rated us
rate of exchange
rate of interest
rates and taxes
rates of interest
rather than

recent information
reduced us
referring to your letter
refer to drawer
registered letter
regret to state
regular attention
regular charges
regular form
regular forms
regular requirements
related business
represent charges
reputable companies
required capital
required subscription
restricted application
restrictive indorsement
Retail Price Index
reversionary interest
right hon. gentleman
right honourable
right or wrong
river embankment

Royal Borough
Royal car
Royal Charter
Royal Family
royal icing
Royal nurse
royal pardon
royal procedure
Royal procession
royal welcome
rushed off
sales manager
Saturday evening
Saturday evenings
Saturday next
school punishment
scientific field
scientific procedure
scientific publication
scientific research
scientific work
Secretary of State
Secretary of State for Scotland
Secretary of State for Wales

seems to have
selected us
sensible arrangements
sensible charges
sensible of the
sensibly arranged
service manager
set forth
several authorities
several ships
several weeks
several yards
severe punishment
she will be instructed
ship's captain
shop manager
shorthand writer
shorthand writing
showed us
showed us the
sign of the times
similar business
similar documents
similar letters

similar objectives
similar reasons
similar results
similar services
similar situations
similar types
six weeks
six weeks' time
social security
social security benefit
Society of Engineers
so forth
Solicitor General
some of those
some of them
some other words
some punishment
some shipments
some yards
so well
so well known
special attention
special charges
specially indorsed

staff colonel
standing order
steam pressure
Stock Exchange
stretched out the
subscription charges
subscription department
subscription form
subscription forms
subscription required
subsidiary companies
such valuations
sufficient insurance
Sunday evening
Sunday evenings
Sunday next
supplementary benefit
supported the beginning
supported us
surprised us
tanker captain
team captain
technical college
technical colleges

technical difficulties
technical difficulty
technical progress
technical terms
telegram charges
telephone bills
Thames Embankment
that government
that is to say
that their abilities
that these shipments
that we have to be instructed
theft insurance
their ability
their application
their government
their own nationals
their valuation
there is no objection
there is no reality
there is the reality
these shipments
these ships
these words
they are not logical
they assure us
they may well have
they were
they will have to say that
third party
this application
this bank
this evening
this government
this house
this information
this morning
this party
this ship
this shipment
this week
this word
those words
thousand words
thousand yards
throughout the world
Thursday evening
Thursday evenings

Thursday morning

Thursday next

to a great extent

to assure

to assure the

to assure you

to be instructed

to be sure

to be the captain

to bring forth

to call forth

to carry on

to carry on the

to face reality

to give forth

to great

to make application

tomorrow evening

too little

too much

too many

too much pressure

to reach policies

to represent the government

to say a few words

to the house

touched us

towards one another

towards the beginning

to work

trade journal

trade mark

travellers' cheques

Treasury Bills

treated us

trust funds

Tuesday evening

Tuesday evenings

Tuesday next

turned out

turning to the balance sheet

turning to the profit and loss account

turn to the balance sheet

two hundred words

two hundred yards

two months

two or three

two thousand words

two weeks
typed out
unchecked bills
uncleared charges
under the circumstances
undoubted assurance
unexpected beginning
United Kingdom
unpaid bills
unused capital
valuation certificate
value added tax
verdict for the defendant
verdict for the plaintiff
very best authorities
very well
very well indeed
volume of business
walked out
warm morning
water mark
water pressure
we are assured
we are informed

we are in receipt of your letter
we are instructed
we are sure
we assure you
we can say
we can see
Wednesday evening
Wednesday evenings
Wednesday next
we expect to receive
we gave
we give
we have no objection
we have pleasure
we have received
we have several yards
we have to say that
well-managed insurance
were there
we shall be glad if you will
we shall be glad to hear
we shall be glad to receive
we thank you for your letter
we told

we were
we were instructed
we would like to say a few words
what is the matter
what you
when you
whenever it may
whenever there has
whenever there has been
whenever they
whenever this
when we were
when we were not
whether it is
whether or not
whether there are
whether we believe
who were
why not
will and testament
will be instructed
will you kindly let me know
winter morning
with best wishes

within the next few months
within the next few weeks
without recourse
with reference to
with reference to which
with regard to
with respect to
worked out the
would you
written application
written authority of the drawer
yes or no
yesterday evening
yesterday morning
you are not logical
you can be assured
you can say
you can see
you may also
you may also be
you may rest assured
young man
young men
young men and women

your ability		your government	
your application		your punishment	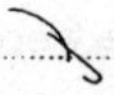
your assurance		your valuation	
your bank		your Worship	
your board	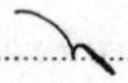	you were	
your directors	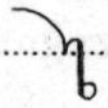		